THE REST IS HISTORY

THE REST IS HISTORY

———

Gerald Dawe

Abbey Press
1998

First published February 1998
Reprinted November 1998

Abbey Press   Abbey Press
Newry Office ◆ *Belfast Office*
Courtenay Hill   24 Martello Park
Newry   Craigavad
County Down   County Down
Northern Ireland   Northern Ireland
BT34 2ED   BT18 0DG

A CIP record for this book is available from the British Library

ISBN: 1 9016 1703 3
Author: Dawe, Gerald
Title: The Rest is History
Format: 138 mm x 214 mm
1998

Design: Adrian Rice
Cover Image: Paul Wilson
Typesetting by David Anderson in 11/13pt Sabon
Printed by Nicholson & Bass Ltd, Belfast

CONTENTS

Acknowledgements

Many friends have encouraged me with this project, in particular Gerry Fanning, John Wilson Foster, Paul Heaney, Thomas Kilroy, Aodán MacPóilin, Michael Mulreany and Jonathan Williams. I am also indebted to Van Morrison who helped me with several details from his prodigious memory. The Rev. Gary Armstrong gave of his time and knowledge and put me right on a series of musical matters and Louise Kidney got the whole thing into shape.

Lyrics quoted in 'The Burning Ground' are courtesy of Van Morrison and Exile Productions.

Acknowledgements are gratefully made to the following where some of this material appeared in its original form: The John Hewitt Summer School, Carnlough, Antrim; Kerry International Summer School, Tralee, Kerry; 'Contemporary Irish Drama and Theatre' Conference, University of Tübingen, Germany; 'The Revision of England' Conference, University of Kingston-upon-Thames, London; The Second Fife and Drum Conference, Shankill, Belfast; *Eire/Ireland* (USA), *Fortnight*, *Honest Ulsterman*, Lagan Press, *New Hibernia Review* (USA), RTE and *The Irish Times*.

GERALD DAWE

for
Iarla and Olwen

You see the point. I want to tell the truth,
and already I have told you about wide rivers.
It should be clear by now that the truth
about the place is elusive, and must be tracked with caution.

Joan Didion

THE REST IS HISTORY

PART ONE

◆

THE BURNING GROUND
Belfast and Van Morrison

I

Coming into Belfast, the capital of Northern Ireland, is like approaching a sunken city. It lies inside a horse-shoe of surrounding hills, the coastal land to its southern shoreline is the rich, undulating landscape of County Down; to Belfast's northerly shores is County Antrim: a harsher, dramatic terrain that faces Scotland across the narrow straits of the sea of Moyle.

Unlike most Irish towns or cities which give their own name to the immediate hinterland – Dublin, Galway, Cork, Sligo, Waterford, Derry, Donegal – Belfast is just itself. The lough at whose mouth the city fans out is fed by the river Lagan, which flows down through the untouched meadows and park forests, along embankments and under the bridges which link the south and east of the city with the north and west.

In the building docks and islands, old quays and wharves, Belfast's industrial history as a shipbuilding and merchant port, makes way for the new transport of ferry terminals. The channels such as Victoria and Musgrave and basins like Pollock which had borne tankers, liners and gunships for the British fleet rub shoulders now with a busy and expanding City airport. The massive gantries of the Harland & Wolff shipbuilders – once the greatest of its kind in the world – straddle the city's horizon like monumental arches.

Clutched around Belfast's inner reaches, the mills and factories, warehouses and engineering works, are isolated by the *svelte* dominance of motorway and bypass.

What remains of Belfast's industrial architecture has a strange marooned look to it. Similarly, the redbrick Gothic of insurance houses and banks, stores and churches, hotels and theatres which was once the city's Victorian legacy has all but vanished. Belfast underwent the fate of many cities in Britain and Ireland caught and mauled by the hectic redevelopment boom of the 1980s. What has taken over, inside out as it were, is the shopping mall, the steel-framed Centre and the masked façade. These changes belie another truth, however, of the profound, irrevocable change Belfast experienced as the site of sectarian violence which took possession of the city from the late 1960s – bombing campaigns in the name of Irish national liberation vied with bombing campaigns in the name of preserving the British way of life. Peace-lines of metal girders divided communities against themselves, security barriers defaced the cityscape and turned the centre into a police zone.

The map of the city is a history of territorial allegiances and tribal loyalties. To quote from Jonathan Bardon's definitive study, *Belfast: An Illustrated History*:

> Whether or not the citizens of Belfast regularly practised their religion, the vast majority unhesitatingly felt themselves either to be protestant or catholic. It was amongst the working-classes that segregation was most complete, especially in Ballymacarrett and the Falls – Shankill region of west Belfast.

For anyone growing up in the Belfast of the late 1940s and '50s there was always going to be an inbred sense of where one literally walked. This sense of place has been grotesquely theatricalised as a result of 'The Troubles' and the physical institutionalisation of sectarian divisions during the 1970s and '80s. But it is true to say that over the generations Belfast people, particularly working-class people, were born with second sight; a radar as to where one was in the city. Lacking such instinct could spell danger in the nighttown life of Belfast and most certainly led to many a harsh word and 'scrap' (or street-fight).

Eventually, the political divisions of the city, crackling like an electric storm, were earthed in precisely these intensely intimate and cross-grained innerlives of the city's myriad neighbourhoods.

In the late 60s and early 1970s, what had once been a 'mixed' area, meaning a neighbourhood where protestant and catholic families had 'got on well', experienced the shock of having to face the truth about Belfast's sectarian divisions. Similarly, the traditional protestant and catholic areas which had previously been negotiable by bus or foot, when leaving a girl home after a dance, or meeting a pal, or going to a party, became increasingly more dangerous and ultimately amounted to a perilous risk upon which few would chance their lives. By the mid-1970s when assassination squads roamed what became known as 'twilight zones', or interfaces between the dominant working-class districts, Belfast had ceased to be a living city and had become, for a decade and more, a ghost town.

Districts played, and still play, a key role in defining the identity of Belfast. Even though there have been extraordinary population shifts within the city over the last twenty-five years, because of intimidation and violence, on the one hand, and redevelopment on the other, the sense of being from a particular area is strong and lasting. It is a pattern common to many industrial cities such as Belfast.

Put at its simplest, Belfast is physically indistinguishable from the industries which were established in the nineteenth and twentieth centuries: linen-mills, ropeworks, tobacco factories, shipbuilding, engineering works.

Erected literally within this formidable industrial landscape were the streets and houses of the workers. It is not physically possible to think about Belfast as if it were different from this industrial past. Consequently, Belfast is unique in Ireland and has much more in common with Liverpool or Glasgow since the pattern of its streets as much as the commercial nature of the city centred on the industrial heartland; little else.

Each district had its own factory and customs linked to the work-practises of the factory; its own destiny, and well-being, tied irrevocably to that factory. The Falls, a predominantly catholic road, had its mills; York Street in the protestant lower northside had the famous Gallaher's tobacco factory while the shipyards dominated the east of the city. It was a pattern replicated throughout the city, layer by layer, from the dockland upwards until the prosperous higher roads circle the outer city and wind into the nearby countryside.

This pattern is rapidly disappearing in the post-industrial 1990s but going back forty years, it was a fact of life that those who grew up in the districts surrounding, or, more like, hugging the industrial shore, would become part of it. The story of their lives was the story of the industries in which they worked. Indeed, one reason for the fierceness of the sectarian passion which has characterised Belfast throughout its history is the struggle to maintain some standard of living in a city whose economy was (and, of course, remains) fundamentally susceptible to the unpredictable diktats of a distant government in Westminster.

What *was* known was the streets where one lived; they were predictable. Families stayed, generation through generation, and while the men in the house (and sometimes the daughters) might follow work 'across the water' (to Britain) or emigrate further afield to Canada or Australia, the home territory was a proven ground. Here the rituals of Belfast life were handed down via the calendar of quasi religious rites and political commemorations.

For the protestant community, in the main identifying themselves with the union with Britain, their sense of being different from the Irish nationalist cultural and political aspirations of the catholic community, was celebrated (in the past) through Orange parades and marches. Taking place annually throughout the summer months of July and August, these parades in Belfast were dramatised statements of territorial imperatives and cultural bonding. If Cork or Limerick had Corpus Christi, Belfast, or those parts which called themselves protestant, had The Twelfth.

The serried ranks of bedecked men, in good suits and bowler hats, with sashes and silver insignias pinned onto armlets and lapels, immaculate white gloves and carrying huge silken banners that swayed like canopies in the wind, was an amazing and quite disturbing sight. Carrying the symbols of the British Crown and Imperial past as if they were religious relics, these men assembled in the back-streets to demonstrate their loyalty to Queen and Faith and Country.

The major roads and avenues into the centre of the town and beyond the city to a field of worship were transformed into a bizarre occasion caught somewhere between the mood of Mardi Gras and the formal opening of a Guild Hall. Meanwhile behind such a contradictory carnival – which included the pagan-like burning of bonfires on the Eleventh Night, the night before the marching took place, and the sombre declaration of protestant religious beliefs – the catholic community either left the city if they could afford to, kept in doors or observed from a safe distance these men and their followers as they sang and danced through large parts of the city, and the city's centre.

Again, much has changed over the years and the power of the Twelfth Marches of the Orange Order has narrowed into an explosively symbolic reminder of the divisions which have underscored the city's history.

From such loci, however, the co-ordinates of life in Belfast were formed. Antenna of curiosity could identify invisible barriers, marking out the social parameters within which people lived. To know *where* someone lived was tantamount to knowing their religion. Received wisdom could then take over.

Moving out from where the City Hall sits inside Donegall Square, the roads and avenues form a compass of religious and cultural division. Rising up out of Donegall Place, Royal Avenue and York Street are the famous districts of the Falls, Shankill and Crumlin: what is now called West Belfast. Turning east towards the Lagan and crossing the river 'over the bridge' are the Newtownards, Albertbridge, Beersbridge and Woodstock districts. The land is densely-housed, each neighbourhood a protectorate all on its own.

The predominantly protestant east of the city is like a triangular wedge, bordered by one of the longest roads in the city – the Newtownards Road – and by the Castlereagh and Knock roads. Within the triangle reside the neighbourhoods of Ballymacarret, Bloomfield, Strandtown, Ballyhackamore, Castlereagh, Cregagh and Orangefield.

The streetscapes are familiar to anyone who has lived in a provincial industrial city. East Belfast in particular was defined by that industrial past since shipbuilding physically dominated the horizon. In a literal and imaginative sense the gantries, sirens, workers' houses and buses; the very sounds and sights of post-war Belfast were determined by the ups and downs of shipbuilding orders at the two great industrial sites of Harland & Wolff and Workman and Clark. 'By 1959', remarks Jonathan Bardon, 'the works covered 300 acres'. Indeed, it may be difficult to appreciate today the extent to which Belfast had once been a leading industrial presence throughout the world. At least three of its industries – shipbuilding, ropeworks and linen – were the largest of their kind at one time or another. Leslie Clarkson looks back to the early years of the twentieth century and sees Belfast's dominance not simply in Irish terms:

> There were a few small shipbuilding and repairing yards in Dublin, Londonderry and elsewhere, but their importance was declining and their output negligible. Belfast's importance was, in fact, greater than simply percentages indicate, for her yards concentrated on big ships for the merchant marine and Royal Navy, not small tramp and coastal steamers. It was around the Belfast shipbuilding industry, and to a lesser extent the textile industry, that the engineering industry clustered. Except for steam-engine manufacture, agricultural machinery, railway engineering and cycle making, Belfast was dominant in all branches of engineering in Ireland, and its textile machinery, in particular, had world-wide renown.

Queen's Island, the symbolic heartland of east Belfast, was the site of the leading shipbuilding business in the world throughout the 1950s. Terence Brown, the cultural historian and literary critic, has accurately defined the parameters of this industrial world in, 'Let's Go To Graceland', a memoir of the east Belfast-born playwright, Stewart Parker:

> On any working morning men poured over the bridge that spanned the Lagan and out of the narrow streets of red brick kitchen houses into the shipyard that still saw itself with the

Clyde [Glasgow] as a world power in that heroic industry. The rope works were the largest in the world and you could believe it watching the shawlies [women factory workers] teeming around its gates as the hooter sounded summoning them to work through the foggy murk of a part of the city that seemed always in semi-darkness. And there was the aircraft factory and aerodrome too.

Shipbuilding, ropeworks, aircraft, linen mills, manufacturing of one kind or another; the allied business of commercial and corporation administration; central and local government; service industries – all had turned Belfast into a thriving industrial post-war city. Precious wonder that from John Keats' description in 1818 of 'passing into Belfast through a most wretched suburb' and hearing 'that most disgusting of all noises . . . the sound of the [linen mill's] shuttle' to Louis MacNeice's poem 'Valediction', the image of Belfast was exclusively one of a city *defined* by work. MacNeice's Thirties Belfast is 'devout and profane and hard':

Built on reclaimed mud, hammers playing in the shipyard,
Time punched with holes like a steel sheet, time
Hardening the faces, veneering with a grey and speckled rime
The faces under the shawls and caps:
This was my mother-city, these my paps.

MacNeice was to change his mind and discover beneath the seemingly unchangeable 'outer ugliness and dourness' a deeper reality which he found upon his regular visits back to the city during the 1950s. But the simple truth of the matter is that modern Belfast was a city founded upon heavy industry, and east Belfast developed out of that cauldron. Such historical reality cannot tell the whole story, nevertheless.

Around the (now defunct) rope and engineering works, streets of parlour and kitchen houses ('two-ups-two-downs') give unto wider roads and avenues, wealthy parks and gardens before becoming the countryside.

This is how Brenda Collins traces the established pattern of housing and civic and visual amenity in the early decades of the twentieth century as Belfast's population rapidly increased:

Its roots were in the early industrial development of the city and the subsequent exodus of the middle and professional classes from their Donegall Square townhouses, whose grandeur had declined as the smoky industrial chimneys increased, to the more spacious and airy suburbs. Doctors and financiers, solicitors and architects now separated their home lives from their professional lives. This movement was most obvious in the south of the city where the middle class suburbs of the Malone ridge and the University area were a much more healthy environment than lower down Dublin Road near the 'nuisance' of the River Blackstaff, which was contaminated by the refuse of mills and factories . . . To the north of the city centre overlooking the shores of Belfast Lough, the former deerpark of the Donegalls was divided into Oldpark and Newpark. Northwards from Carlisle Circus areas such as Mount Vernon, Parkmount and Duncairn and the loughside estates of the Grove, Fortwilliam and Skegoniel grew from the parcelling out of villa parkland into attractive sites for the aspiring lower middle class of commercial clerks and manufacturers' agents . . . Across the Lagan, beyond industrial Ballymacarett and Lagan village, a vigorous suburban development was also under way, and the estates of Ormeau, Ravenhill, Rosetta, Annadale, Knock, Belmont and Stormont were gradually replaced by neat avenues and parades of new villas.

The significance of these distinctions should not be lost to us. Belfast clearly was, and still is, a civic landscape of class distinction. 'The pattern', writes political historian Patrick Buckland, 'was established well before partition but became more pronounced afterwards as a result of intimidation in "times" of crisis and the pressure of local politics'. Buckland goes on:

In the former instance, families of the 'wrong sort' were driven out of their homes or considered it advisable to leave, while local politicians were concerned to maintain if not enlarge their majorities by the careful allocation of houses among electoral areas. Segregation was most marked in Belfast. The Falls became almost exclusively catholic, as catholics of all social groups moved into the area, which in the nineteenth century had been a working class preserve. As a necessary corollary, the main protestant districts became

even more homogeneous, although without the same
admixture of classes.

The final clause in Patrick Buckland's last sentence is
particularly revealing here. While 'protestant districts' were
'even more homogeneous' in terms of religious affiliation than
their catholic counterpoints in other parts of the city, there
was not 'the same admixture of classes'. What in effect
Buckland is alluding to is the important housing differences as
working-class housing bordered upon lower-middle-class
housing which in turn bordered upon middle-class housing
and so on. A class-conscious, incremental, tier-system, in other
words. Streetscapes altered, widened and opened out the
further one moved up and away from the city-basin and its
immediate hinterland. From a very early age, Belfast children
learned their place in this scheme of things based largely upon
their physical surroundings; assimilating architectural and
civic barriers of class as much as absorbing, and sometimes,
rejecting, or transcending as best they could, the discreet signs
of religious – and hence, political identity. Accents, too, played
a specific, instructive role in deciding within seconds one's
background. For working-class kids who lived in what would
approximate today to 'the inner city', the 'posh areas' were
merely a step away, in one sense, and, in another, a whole
world away. To know one's own place was both a source of
strength but also a terrible inhibition.

It was often out on weekend walks through these avenues
and parks that one saw the different styles of life counterposed
quite starkly with one's own. Houses like mansions; tree-lined
driveways; gardens like parks. Sedate, discreet, private. A
landscape of imaginative thresholds amounted to a metaphor
of the imagination itself. Yet within the intimate, even
claustrophobic closeness of the working-class districts there
were the random open spaces of builders' yards, fugitive rivers
and streams, old warehouses, industrial networks and vast
walls.

For a young boy or girl, part of 'a gang of mates', life
growing up in such a district was like a pendulum-swing

between adventure and boredom, dreaming and routine, desire crossing against the force of custom, expectation and convention.

Things were close at hand: local cinemas and shops, school and church, sport and clubs, bars and walks – all available within the community. The outside world, whether that be London or America, lived in the imagination, fed by film, or the radio, or magazines, or letters and parcels from an uncle or aunt; one of the displaced family.

After the ravages of World War II, Belfast, like so many other cities which had experienced at first hand the reality of war – the Blitz of 1941 had left over 700 dead and whole areas of the city destroyed – was busy trying to come to terms with peace.

But the city had been exposed, in a storm of outrage, blame and shame, to the fact that many of its citizens had been living in appalling housing conditions. Furthermore, the Blitz, having forced tens of thousands from the city, presented startling evidence of the evacuees' poor state of health.

The late 1940s and 50s mark a time when practical solutions to *some* of these problems were attempted, particularly in the field of housing, health and education. What did not change, however, was the basic religious and political demographic fault-lines of the city. Some voices predicted trouble ahead if these deepseated and by now visible grievances of the ordinary people were not addressed.

Yet, according to historian Jonathan Bardon, for the citizens of Belfast, 'the Second World War had been far more harrowing that the First' but now 'the sense of optimism and hope seemed stronger than in 1918; to a large extent this was justified'.

II

Born in 1945 (August 31st) to George Morrison and Violet Stitt, Ivan George Morrison's early years follow a traditional pattern, at least on the surface. The surname in Ulster draws together the province's Gaelic roots. According to Robert Bell, Morrison is among 'the thirty most numerous names in Scotland' while its Irish origin as O'Muirgheasain (from Muirgheas meaning 'sea valour') is in County Donegal, the most westerly of the Ulster counties. Indeed the exchange and cross-fertilisation between Ulster and Scotland are imbedded in the Morrison name itself. As Robert Bell explains, a branch of the Donegal O'Morrison's migrated at some unknown date from Inishowen 'to Lewis and Harris in the Scottish Isles' where some 'became bards to the MacLeods'.

In *Scottish Clans and Tartans*, Ian Grimble elaborates upon the Morrisons as a clan of Scandinavian extraction, their founder being a natural son of the King of Norway, cast ashore on the Scottish island of Lewis.

> A legend tells that [the Morrisons] were first ship-wrecked . . . so that their clan badge is driftwood. Clan genealogies trace their descent from Somerled, the King of the Isles who died in 1164 and probably descended from the Celto-Norse King of Ireland . . . One of the most memorable Morrisons of Lewis is Ruaraidth (or Roderick in its anglicised form) who was born there in about 1660. He is remembered as *An Clarsail Dall*, the Blind Piper, and in fact he holds the highest place in the traditions of his country . . . 'Oran Mor Mhic Leoid' [is] surely one of the most beautiful of Gaelic laments. In it he not only mourned the death of his patron at Dunvegan, but also the passing of the old Celtic culture there under his anglicised successor.

Other references to Morrison pick out the overlapping connections, historically and culturally, between Ulster and Scotland, and mythopoetically with Scandinavia, while running consistently through such sources there is the recurring element of music and poetry:

> John Morrison was the author of *Dain spioradail*, 1828 and Iain Morrison, the poetic blacksmith of Rodel, died in 1852.

No matter how one views the veracity of family trees, the unmistakable cultural and social meshing of his own surname provides a myth of origin which Morrison would explore in his music. Precious wonder too that his famous 1973–74 band and production company, *Caledonia* should take its meaning from the Latin for northern Britain and refers to a native of ancient Scotland. The cultural voyage which Morrison undertook in the early 1970s was in effect a journey back in time to such mythical beginnings.

At the age of five Van Morrison went to Elm Grove Primary School, a stone's throw away from his home at 125 Hyndford Street, just off the Beersbridge Road. The school banked on to Lady Dixon's playing fields; across the road, a clutch of streets with such pastoral names as Avoneil and Flora, and the historically laden Mayflower, while the Conn's Water ran through the district as a reminder of an earlier time when it gave its name to a small coastal port of some importance in the late sixteenth and seventeenth centuries.

Ballymacarret, the townland, takes its name from the Gaelic, and means *Town of MacArt*. It is a staunchly protestant and loyalist area. Orange halls, band halls, working-men's clubs and bars and more recently, leisure and day centres, nursery schools and shopping malls front the redeveloped housing estates which settle alongside the numerous places of worship: Church of Ireland, Presbyterian, Methodist, Baptist, Non-Conformist and several evangelical sects such as Elim Pentecostal.

Morrison, like most of his contemporaries went to Sunday school and church. In the grand St Donard's Church of Ireland at the Bloomfield intersection, barely ten minutes walk from the leafy Cypress Avenue and suburban North Road, the setting for some of his great early lyrics, Morrison would have heard an austere lesson in Christian faith, duty and reserve. Whereas in the evangelical meetings, an energetic and Americanised version of the gospel would speak of a spirited mission of redemption, the Blood of the Lamb and joy in Christ.

Protestantism was everywhere. From the Union Jack flying above the Orange halls, to billboards proclaiming Proverbial wisdom from the Bible, assemblies and religious instruction at school, it was impossible *not* to absorb the teaching and cultural values of the protestant church. In working-class east Belfast, as in other working class areas throughout the city, protestantism was a very wide church indeed, embracing mainstream traditions such as Anglicanism, Presbyterianism and Methodism towards the distinctively evangelical.

Protestants often took an *à la carte* attitude to their worship. While membership of a particular church passed down through families, generation by generation, it was not uncommon for mothers, in particular, to shop around and send their children to different churches under the broad umbrella of protestantism.

There was the 'respectable' Church of Ireland, a hint always of the upwardly mobile seeking a place alongside the satisfied burghers of the district; the down-to-earth Presbyterians who tended also towards the political; the somewhat introverted Methodists and a panoply of different sects and breakaway groups who asked for much more personal commitment from their flock. 'There is in Ulster', remarks Steve Bruce, 'a *pietistic* evangelical tradition which sees religion as an alternative to the ways of the world and which stresses the importance of avoiding worldly contamination. Especially strong in working-class areas, a gospel-hall and Pentecostal tradition serves as a way out of the everyday world'.

The atmosphere of such gospel halls and evangelical meeting houses could not be more different from either the highbred Churches of Ireland or the Presbyterian Scottish Gothick. Built on wastelands, in derelict sites of one kind or another, at corners and out-of-the way places, the huts of the evangelical revivalist preachers attracted a small but steady flow of the curious and disenchanted. Over the years, such sects developed and grew; the faithful paid for and built tabernacles in which fully flown crusades took place along with open-air rallies.

It is interesting to note that the best-known evangelical preacher to come out of Northern Ireland, Ian Paisley, preached an invitation sermon on Christmas Sunday 1945 at the Ravenhill Evangelical Mission Church in working-class east Belfast before becoming pastor to that Church. Within his lifetime he was to create a new church, the Free Prebysterian Church, one of whose buildings straddles the Ravenhill Road and receives busloads of worshippers every week.

That said, the sects are, and always have been, a minority in Belfast. Among the working-class, such sects are often seen as obsessive, dour and self-righteous. Their influence fades into the wider Calvinist atmosphere which pervaded the city throughout the post-war period and well into the Sixties. There was a governing ethos of Sabbatarian rule, when all forms of entertainment were frowned upon on a Sunday – public bars, clubs, parks, cinemas and (most) dancehalls were closed; television was not allowed; blinds were often pulled or curtains closed and it was considered improper to play on the streets. The lasting negative effects of such a puritanical society upon those who grew up in it are obviously profound and mark to the very core the individual sensibility. There is, however, another side to this story. For the dominant religious force of protestantism also carried, in different forms again, a contradictory sense of poetic language and choral and lyrical music.

While the routines of an evangelical meeting might appear to be soulless in comparison with, say, the ceremony of catholic Mass or the pomp of High Church, the language of 'being healed' and 'saved', the plain witness of one man's voice bearing testimony to finding the Lord, has a poignancy and theatricality all its own. Largely based upon the Old Testament, adamant in its fundamentalist convictions of right and wrong, sin and forgiveness, speaking out against self-deception, and seeking the Lord through being Born Again, the language and performance of such preachers provided as much entertainment as it did spiritual guidance. The Minister, or pastor, or preacher, brings his religion to the audience so that they might see the light and error of their ways, and gain thereby a new security of whom and what they are, having found themselves through salvation.

The evangelical power of conversion and redemption is drenched in the imagery of a simpler life, spurning illusions and the allure of false gods. It is a forceful, dogmatic and profoundly individualistic faith which earnestly wrestles with issues of 'Truth' and the pursuit of the transcendental as both are embodied in the everyday, working life.

Hardly surprising then that the district Morrison grew up in should include a Calvin Street. Protestantism was after all not solely 'a religion' but the way of life. As Morrison's ironic understatement has it: 'We didn't go to church all the time, but it was a very churchy atmosphere in the sense that that's the way it is in Northern Ireland'.

If protestantism was like the air one breathed, the ground one walked on was assumed to be *British*. Post-war Belfast was an emphatically British city. Belfast had a recent history in common with other British cities – from the war effort to the Blitz and the thousands of American GIs, to the Victory Parades, ration-books, while the city itself was marked with bomb-sites and pre-fabricated houses.

There were the local connections with Scotland – geographical as much as industrial – and the politico-economic associations and cultural identification between a majority of the protestant community and the mainland, and a not insubstantial proportion of the catholic community as well.

Leaving for work in Scotland and England (but less so in Wales) was part of the Belfast way-of-life. There was the historical exchange within the British Isles as job opportunities fell inside the Ulster province and rose elsewhere. Men would travel and settle, sometimes taking their families with them; sometimes not. This 'internal' emigration with family members eventually establishing homes away from Belfast – in Glasgow, London, Leeds, Birmingham, Newcastle, Liverpool – was a fairly common practise since quite early on in the century and indeed, before then as well. In my own family, for instance, one grandfather moved to Canada and worked for many years there before moving to Nottingham; his wife's sister left Belfast in the 1920s and settled in London, only to return once every ten years, and her daughter left London in the 1960s, lived and worked in Belfast for some time before returning to London. Such journeying back and forth has followed personal needs and at the same time reflected the wider economic and cultural pressures over the past century. This 'emigration' accelerated at various critical moments such as the Depression of the late 1920s and mid to late Thirties with emigration further afield to Canada, America and Australia. More recently, from the early 1970s to the present, the twenty-five years of the 'Troubles', has seen an exodus particularly among the young.

It was not always thus, however. Workers could also travel into Northern Ireland, although it was a protected labour market, given the scandalously high unemployment figures of the province. Permits were required for anyone born outside to work inside. Be that as it may, there was a constant flow of workers back and forth across the Irish sea. I recall meeting in 1986 at a Christmas party in suburban north London the Scottish father of a very English hostess. He was in his eighties and had worked, he told me with ironic pride, on the building of Stormont, the Northern Ireland parliament buildings which were opened in 1932 by the then Prince of Wales and later Edward VIII.

The imposing neo-classical house of colonial parliament, visible from over much of Belfast, dominates an impressively landscaped site on the Upper Newtonards Road in the east of the city. The old worker told me that there were many Scottish craftsmen who worked on the building, having been brought in especially from Glasgow, including goldleaf specialists whose artwork, originally used for the grand interiors of liners, can still be seen on the ceilings and cornices of this once all-powerful seat of provincial power.

Stormont's extended heyday was between 1932 and 1972 when the British Prime Minister, Edward Heath, suspended the Stormont government as a result of the rapidly deteriorating security and political situation in Northern

Ireland to address the religious and cultural divisions that were most potently marked in the north. While the economic basis of the state was deeply indebted to British investment, so also were its educational and social welfare systems underwritten by the British government in Westminster.

For barely twenty years or so, in the post-World War II, pre-Troubles period, (roughly between the late 1940s and late 1960s) the provincial government had within its grasp the opportunity to redress the sense of injustice and discrimination many catholics experienced throughout Northern Ireland, and in no place more keenly, than Belfast. That failure of political will was undeniably the key historical turning point. It acted like a catalyst to the sectarian warfare, political jingoism and paramilitary power struggles which would eventually claim the lives of over three thousand people and maim, physically and emotionally, hundreds of thousands of people in the north, the Republic , in Britain and elsewhere.

Yet most historians agree that the slow signs of prosperity which started to show in the local post-war northern economy (with the shipyard employing 20,000 workers in 1959, as against 2000 in 1994) and the steps being taken to better the living standards of ordinary people, were all linked in the public mind at least with the continued union of Northern Ireland with Britain. School-books, radio programmes, and regional television when it eventually came (May 1955) accepted and underscored the status quo. There was an unquestionable relief that Belfast had weathered the storm and that it could look forward, in some manner of means, to an improved future, certainly if measured by pre-war standards.

A new health system was inaugurated and in 1947 the Education Act established, amongst other items, free public secondary-intermediate education. This would take all children from 5 to 15 years of age. The grammar school sector expanded somewhat to cope with the rising lower middle-class aspirations and further education centres opened.

To a young boy, moving between home, school and just knocking around, such concerns were irrelevant. It seems clear that to Van Morrison the main preoccupation of his childhood years was music. This would not have been uncommon either.

Throughout working-class Belfast different forms of music proliferate, particularly in terms of playing music of one traditional form or another. Often associated with ceremonial occasions, a tradition exists of flute-bands, silver-bands, military bands which filled the air not only during the marching seasons of July and August but throughout the year as well. Band practise was an accepted and regular meeting place, and remains an extensive tradition subject to very little research but much misunderstanding.

For the Orange party tunes – like the rebel songs of the Nationalist tradition – form only *one* part, and a greatly fluctuating part, in the tradition as a whole. The tunes of these different kinds of bands vary greatly from hymns to ballads to popular music (title-tracks from television programmes, for example,) to marching tunes.

The principle of selection has generally been what is popular at any given time, along with the ceremonial music drawn from the British military tradition: from 'Rock of Ages' to 'Z Cars' to a Beatles number to 'The Dam Busters' to a sentimental Percy French melody for good measure.

As the Rev. Gary Hastings, an authority on northern musical traditions, explained to me, the great desire of late nineteenth and twentieth century northern protestant marching music was for respectability; a demonstration of community discipline and self-regard modelled along military lines.

Having moved from the infantryman's fife-and-drum to the civilian flute, snaredrum, Scottish pipes, accordion, (and more rarely, the powerful lambeg drum) the band music provided a cultural backdrop to life in Northern Ireland. Its message was double-edged: on the one hand, it was simply music to be played for its own sake and heartily enjoyed. On the other hand, it was 'protestant' music insofar as it maintained, on particular public and state occasions, cultural distinctions between that community and their fellow catholic northerners. It was a music played on the streets and in the parks; broadcast on the radio and featured in church. Indeed, as Gary Hastings pointed out, the role of the church is central in maintaining public interest in ceremonial music. For in one protestant church, or church hall, after another, religion and entertainment met.

Furthermore, through the socialising role of its own organisations, such as the Boys' and Girls' Brigade, the Scouting Movement and so forth, the language, imagery and morality of Bible, Faith and Empire meshed into one common fabric. The church, in other words, was a social place and music played an absolutely crucial role in unifying the community.

Again there are differences within the broad protestant faith. As the Rev. Hastings described it, the upbeat, clapping, and religious come-all-ye's of the evangelical fundamentalist sects, which grew out of Ulster, contrast sharply with the Church of Ireland, and its organ-based, choral hymn-singing and remote and thoughtful rituals.

At a much more practical level, of course, with so many bandsmen and bandswomen in the community as a whole – for the catholic community responded with its own orders, religious and cultural societies, and their own bands and days of celebration – the pool of musicians with basic playing skills and knowledge of music was quite extensive, in proportion to the actual population of Belfast and the province at large.

This dominant civic music, powerful and popular as it has been throughout the brief history of the Northern Ireland state, could not totally eclipse 'the tiny musical survivals' (the phrase is the Rev. Hasting's) of an older tradition, a folk music. This technically astute and intensive music, played on the fiddle, flute, melodeon, uilean pipes, bodhran, was basically *dancing* music. When sung, it usually retold sad stories of love-lost, emigration or praise for a beloved local place.

It is an exciting music, driven by powerful but simple repetitive rhymes. Unlike the, relatively speaking, mass involvement of marching bands, the individual fiddler, flute-player or piper addresses a closed audience of fellow-musicians, listeners or a set of dancers. Even the formal concert setting seems unnatural.

The roots of the music are rural and before the advent of radio or television traditional music was *the* form of musical entertainment. But with the explosion of musical options which came in the wake of World War II and the much wider availability of radio, cinema, and eventually television, the tradition went underground. Individual musicians scattered, often in search of work in the cities, in Ireland, Britain and North America. Like blues-guitarists and musicians, if they travelled away from home, they either fell silent or kept within their own ethnic communities. Audiences at home shrank as the new forms of orchestrated popular music took over in the late 1940s and 1950s.

Ciaran MacMathuna, a leading collector of Irish folk music, reminds us of the time when in Ireland, 'middle-class people laughed at this kind of [traditional] music, when it was considered just good enough for the countryside, and when city people and the middle class didn't like or didn't want to know about this music.' Back in the '50s and '60s, MacMathuna recalls, 'on a long dance late in the night, [the band] might have thrown in an Irish dance for a bit of a laugh, but that was all'.

Belfast was different in that, during the early '60s, as the twenty-four year old Morrison described it in an interview published in *Rolling Stone* in July 1970, there was an important, if limited, cross-over taking place in the city:

> Memphis Slim has been in Belfast; Jessie Fuller, Champion Jack Dupree, John Lee Hooker's been there. They've got folk clubs and rock clubs there, but it's got nothing to do with the English scene. In fact, I'd go so far as to say it doesn't have much to do with the Irish scene either, it's just Belfast. It's got its own identity, it's got its own people . . . it's just a different race, a different breed of people. There's a lot of changes there, too. Like the Mc Peak[e]'s on one hand, and some others of us on the other hand, and they're open to all kinds of music, not just one thing. Maybe a third of the people that are into R & B would go to hear the Mc Peak[e]s.

Morrison has also referred in other interviews to his having started off 'in folk music' which can be taken as shorthand for the singer/musician as an individual who first learns and then puts his or her individual stamp on what has gone before. A further interesting note from the 1970 interview is Morrison seeing blues and traditional Irish music as essentially linked in the context of Belfast in the previous decade. The imaginative shift from Irish traditional music to blues and jazz that seemed quite natural in Morrison's recollection of the late 50s and early 1960s had begun to bear political strains by the early 1970s.

Morrison's good fortune was to have encountered traditional Irish music without the politico-cultural freight it was expected to deal with during the next twenty years and more.

More importantly, though, there was the very early exposure to what Morrison has continuously acknowledged as the key influence of his early years in Belfast: his father. 'There was probably only 10 big collectors [of blues and jazz] in Belfast and [my father] was one of them'. Another key figure in the musical life of Belfast, 'one of the pioneers' as Morrison described him in *Hot Press* (1978) was Solly Lipsitz. His record shop, Atlantic Records in the city's High Street, played a pivotal role in making available during the 1950s the entire range of jazz and blues. (A little later, Dougie Knight would fill the same role and later still, for a new generation in Belfast, Terri Hooley's *Good Vibrations* became a conduit for promoting different musical talent.)

Alongside those recordings played to the young Morrison, he has spoken about his mother's singing – 'I'll take you home Kathleen', 'Sweet Sixteen' and 'Irene Goodnight' – as well as the popular ballads of the day. 'Whatever was on the radio'. It was coincidental, of course, that during the 1950s Britain was experiencing a skiffle and trad jazz revival, inspired in part by the Blues played by American blacks. Morrison has often cited his days playing 'in a skiffle group' and his having 'started off in folk music'. The historical picture has been drawn in detail by musicologists such as Charlie Gillet in *The Sound of the City*, Lawrence Cohn in *Nothing But the Blues* and by participants like George Melly in *Revolt into Style*.

Belfast was no exception, and many of the leading lights of the trad jazz revival played concerts in Belfast during the mid to late 1950s. Witness, for example, the English poet, Philip Larkin, who lived and worked as a librarian at Queen's University, as he recalls in the introduction to his record diary *All What Jazz* (1968) the following scene in the Plaza ballroom, Chichester Street, Belfast. It is 1954:

> A thousand people squashed into the smallish Plaza dance hall and a thousand more milled outside, the more enterprising getting in through a small square window in the men's lavatory . . . Lonnie Donegan would come forward with his impersonation of Leadbelly.

Nine year old Morrison was back home in Hyndford Street listening to the original records of Leadbelly and not the impersonation. It is an important distinction to make too because Morrison has identified Leadbelly as one of the strongest earliest influences upon him, along with, somewhat later, other great blues artists such as Muddy Waters, Sonny Terry and Brownie Mc Ghee. The influence, in other words, of these blues singers and musicians came directly through hearing their voices and music, not mediated through popularised versions of them.

George Melly's point in *Revolt into Style* is well worth bearing in mind when he writes about the violent world of which Leadbelly sang. 'Leadbelly was in prison twice on murder charges and had a near psychopathic personality. Donegan's version was safely distanced from that world. Its violence and harshness was make-believe and in retrospect he sounds more like George Formby than Huddie Ledbetter'.

The connection made at such an early age might also account for the emphasis which Morrison had alluded to in interviews with the emotional bonds and cultural aspirations many Belfast people shared with North America as much as with Britain.

In the early 1950s, Morrison's father visited America, worked there for a time and considered moving his wife and son. It was also during this period that Morrison has said he became hooked to the radio, listening to *Voice of America* and clearly the young Morrison's exposure at such an early age to real blues could only have a profound and lasting effect.

It is well worth noting the afterglow in Belfast of the 1950s left by the many American troops, including black GIs, who had been stationed throughout the north. Having brought with them not only bubble-gum and cigarettes but their own styles of music and dance, they took over the floor of ballrooms such as the Plaza (built in 1942) with, for Belfast, an uncharacteristic flamboyance and glamour.

Undoubtedly the Belfast that Morrison knew growing up was split-levelled. There was the orthodox, self-satisfied official exterior, as formidable as the City Hall itself, expecting its citizens to believe that all was well and that things could only get better, particularly for the city's loyal sons and daughters.

On the other hand, there was also throughout the city men and women such as George and Violet Morrison, and their son, Ivan, whose primary interest was simply in music. It was an alternative world which ultimately permeated the pieties and structure of the known and accepted society, experiencing as it then was, in the mid-50s, an upswing and expansion.

One of the new schools established in 1957 and officially opened the following year (May 3rd, 1958) was Orangefield Boy's School. It was subsequently joined by a Girls School and on the same site, by Grosvenor Grammar school.

Orangefield's headmaster was a dynamic yet cool-tempered scholar called John Malone.

He was a liberal who had fought against the staid and complacent educational authorities in Belfast of the time. He sought to build in Orangefield a genuinely comprehensive education for working-class children of east Belfast.

The school curriculum, however, was to include not only the standard grounding in applied trades and clerkly professions that most, if not all, of its students would eventually join. It also set out to encourage a wider – some would say, experimental – learning in music, theatre, politics, and, of course, sport. The school would also provide a social focus.

Malone's vision was supported by the school's young and more experienced teachers alike. His beliefs were, however, to be severely tested given the deepseated cultural prejudices of the 1950s and early 1960s. Work was considered to be the logical and only reason for educating ordinary working class boys and girls. This was in keeping with the dominant religious and political ethos of protestant unionism of the time as well. Orangefield conceded, indeed actively endorsed, these principles in naming the four school 'houses' – or fraternities – after local engineering works such as Sirocco and Bryson.

However, as the school soon established itself by the mid-1960s, it had achieved an academic recognition beyond the original remit and throughout the Sixties was identified as Belfast's leading 'comprehensive' school, with pupils of quite diverse backgrounds attending from all over the city, alongside those drawn from the immediate catchment area of east Belfast. We catch a glimpse of this fission when Morrison describes his years at Orangefield (1956-1960):

> There was no school for people like me. I mean, we were freaks in the full sense of the word because either we didn't have the bread to go to the sort of school where we could sit down and do our thing, or that type of school didn't exist. Most of what was fed me really didn't help me that much later.

While things were to change at that very school in a matter of a few years, Morrison had moved on by then. Given, however, the conservatism and civic priorities of Belfast in the mid-to-late 1950s it is hardly surprising that Morrison, along with others of his own age, should look for something else. Blues music became that voice of dissent but it was fundamentally an emotional reaction, and not a political act. Black musicians like Leadbelly, Jelly Roll Morton and jazz figures like Charlie Parker embodied a way of life and represented a kind of lifestyle with which the young Morrison could identify.

From early on, he had picked up a guitar bought for him by his father. Armed with his guitar Morrison obviously found himself, as so many others of that time and since, with his own fate literally in his hands. Within no time, he was playing and imitating the records he had been listening to and looking for the chance to perform. The crucial difference with Morrison, as the years between the late 1950s and 1967 when he left Belfast clearly show, is that he was not only discovering a powerfully committed talent; he was also encountering the world through his music and its subculture. If playing music was just a job, as he had repeatedly said, it was some job:

> The original idea in the British Isles was just to get out of your working-class environment and make a living out of playing music. It's that simple. I just wanted to be a musician, full-time. That was the ultimate goal (Q. 1993).

Precious wonder that in his later work, of the 1980s and 90s, Morrison would seek to imaginatively rediscover through his music again that early home from whence it had all started. The mature Morrison's realisation is chastened, however, by the fact that it was his very talent which had cast him out in the first place.

Morrison's lyrics are driven by such a sense of contradiction: the intimacy and quietude of home is shaken by doubt and uncertainty about its ability to sustain the demands of the artistic and professional world beyond. Morrison's work as musician, singer and poet negotiates this tension whether that be in the intensely lyrical passages of *Astral Weeks* (1967), the rage of the classic track 'Listen to the Lion' (1974), *Hymns to the Silence* (1991), or *The Healing Game* (1996).

For young men like Morrison seeking work, there was the traditional east Belfast route, apprenticed to one of the local engineering works such as Musgrave & Co. When this proved unsatisfactory, Morrison worked in a meat-cleaning factory, in a chemist's shop and went freelance, cleaning windows around the Orangefield area. Each job was secondary to the real business of playing with the ever-changing line-ups of local bands, from Deanie Sands and The Javelins, later The Thunderbolts, to their latest formation in 1960 when they became The Monarchs. His professional career can be said to start from the early gigs with The Monarchs with whom he played saxophone.

The popular musical background throughout Ireland at this time in the early 60s, north and south, was the public dominance of dancehall showbands, antiseptic ceili music and pub-based folk, modelled on and derived from groups like the Clancy Brothers. The showband scene was an ersatz mixture of cover versions of 'pop' hits from America and England.

Whatever about his private education in blues and jazz, Morrison had to work his way through the audience expectations of the time. The fall-out of the trad-jazz revival in the 50s had more or less petered out and it had returned to minority status, along with Irish traditional music and folk singing.

There was, however, an additional pressure in that Morrison was starting to make connections through his reading with the work of the Beat generation, in particular the iconic autobiographical novel, *On the Road* (1958) written by Jack Kerouac.

Kerouac's fiction, such as *On the Road* and *The Dharma Bums* (1959), dramatise roads to freedom as the group of fugitives spurn the white, puritanical, work-obsessed post-war America of their own time for a life of self-obsessed experiment and indeterminate future on the west coast.

Kerouac also wrote aggressively in his own voice, a style of conversational address, buoyed up with jazz-talk and immediate access to poetic vision:

> It was a wonderful night. Central City is two miles high; at first you get drunk on the altitude, then you get tired, and there's a fever in your soul. We approached the lights around

the opera house down the narrow dark street; then we took a
sharp right and hit some old saloons with swinging doors.
Most of the tourists were in the opera. We started off with a
few extra-size beers. There was a player piano. Beyond the
back door was a view of mountainsides in the moonlight. I
let out a yahoo. The night was on.

For the intense teenager, hanging out in Belfast, these
words must have sounded like a new gospel. As George Jones
a leading musician of the time, remarked: 'He wrote poetry. It
was deep . . . most of us didn't know what he was talking
about'. Kerouac's reverence for jazz, too, would not have gone
amiss, as black blues' artists and the mention of poet figures
such as Rimbaud could only inspire Morrison in undoubtedly
the same way as it had earlier influenced Bob Dylan and The
Doors singer, Jim Morrison, among an entire generation who
were discovering Kerouac for the first time.

It is of course all too easy with hindsight to see in those
first few years of the 1960s Morrison gathering into himself
the professional experience needed to maintain a 'career' as a
musician. Much more importantly, he was forming the
attitudes and belief in himself that such a life was actually
possible. There can be no inevitability about such desires, as if
Morrison planned his career step by step. Far from it. He
moved where and when he could and took what chances came
his way. It is something which Morrison himself has been
quite clear about:

Picture the situation. Put yourself working in showbands,
touring in buses with seven or eight people, sleeping in
parks, having no money. Put yourself through working the
clubs in Germany, on up to when the r'n'b movement thing
was happening in the 60s; put yourself through being in a
situation where you're supposed to be a somebody. The
thing that has carried me through this is the time I put in
when I was nobody. When I was with Them, it was anti-
climactic. All right so I'm a star but I don't want it. I just do
my music.

In an effort to secure more gigs the five-man Monarchs
added four musicians to their original line-up and became a

showband. This meant that while they were no longer 'a group' they could now play in the bigger Belfast ballrooms. The four-piece band (drums, bass, lead guitar and singer) were supplemented with keyboards and brass instruments.

One of the new additions, Ronnie Osborne had joined from a brass band. The Monarchs were in effect caught between two worlds and the next year and more tells a fascinating story of musical aspirations confronting show-business reality. The ballroom requirements were simple: play the music that the audience was hearing on the radio and buying records of in the shops. They were there to dance; the band was there to entertain. After all, dancing was a night out. The top ballrooms themselves were imitation palaces; the showbands were dressed up in distinctive monogrammed liveries (a Crown for The Monarchs) that fell somewhere between quasi-military uniforms (underlined by the somewhat mechanical dance-steps on stage) and formal wedding attire. The showbands also provided flashes of showmanship within an ongoing, self-contained and predictable musical set. The music was all about polish and the majority of the musicians were skilled in imitating all sorts of music. Their inner musical inclinations were quite firmly subservient to the wishes of the audience, ballroom owner and promoter. While some 'hotter' numbers could be smuggled in to become breathing spaces between dances, or to show off one of the band's players, in the main they replicated 'hits', irrespective of whether they were pop, country 'n' western or 'jokey' ballads:

> May the bird of paradise fly up your nose;
> May an elephant caress you with its toes.

As George Jones told journalist Vincent Power, 'There was no other outlet'. Morrison's own comments underscore the commercial realities of the time:

> You couldn't work properly if you didn't have [a horn section]. All the showbands had horn sections and a lot of them were really good, like the Royal Showband, the Dixielanders, the Swingtime Aces, Clipper Carlton.

So what the Monarchs were doing in 1960, ahead of time, was including in their repertoire, alongside the pop material, some material from the r'n'b American style of Ray Charles and Muddy Waters. Such innovation was a risky business but frustrating nonetheless for Morrison who obviously wanted to push further into that terrain.

After a spell away from The Monarchs, Morrison and the by-now seven-piece band, decided to have a go and travelled to Scotland in 1962. Behind them there was five years or so of playing the dance-halls and ballrooms of their own locality – Belfast and the surrounding counties. Now they had left this behind them, albeit only in Scotland, the harsher realities of being away from home, on the road and looking for work must have pressed in upon the unlikely group of lads.

It is a story told many times since of prospecting, buoyed up with the two Glaswegians whom they had met in Belfast. The Belfast group travelled around Scotland expecting more work than they could actually find, and so they decided to travel south to London.

This is the stuff of myth-making, of course: the provincial encounter with the cosmopolitan culture which was such a defining feature of the period that was to become known as the Swinging Sixties': pop culture, literature, film and theatre.

As George Jones recounts, they drove directly to London from Aberdeen: 'We were really tired. We just kept driving to try and find a place to bunk down. We felt dejected. We were ready to go home, but didn't want to give in to our parents.' All teenagers, The Monarchs were in London in 1962 in a van. What they had going for them was their own selves and the knowledge and feeling for a different kind of music. It was to sustain the group for a year or so, including a tour of Britain and Germany, before their return to Belfast in 1963. This was an absolutely crucial time for Morrison's development as an artist because between these years (1962-67) he would be confronted by both the commercial exigencies of the music *business* but also begin the real struggle for his own artistic independence, an abiding theme of his work ever since.

For Morrison records at the very heart of his work a series of dilemmas. He has spoken of these in the interviews he has given throughout a career which now spans more than thirty years, interviews which reveal Morrison as a vastly experienced and uncompromising critic of the contemporary world and the fate within it of genuine artistic endeavour.

As a musician, all Morrison need do is entertain (what he calls 'earning my living') but there is also a profound desire to communicate 'more' than that; as a performer, there is the conflict between protecting the individual private self while dealing with, and in, a mass market music business which thrives on, and exploits, disclosure. There is, too, the never-ending struggle for balance as Morrison's music aspires to some form of genuine spiritual experience while simultaneously contending with the rigours, routines and business of touring a band. Running through these emotionally-charged and intently artistic issues, Morrison's writing lights upon the imagery of protestant mysticism while the songs, reaching for rapture, recollect human limitation and loss against which his voice and lyrics protest.

III

Morrison's time with Them was the brief use of direct musical force. The band, formed in Belfast late in 1963, captured the mood of the city. Indeed from this period in the early 1960s, Belfast was to produce a number of bands who played a mix of r'n'b and blues. They lived on stage-performances, as Morrison has made clear many times, at such venues as Belfast's Maritime Hotel. As a live band, the energy of their performances was not captured in the recording studio – singles such as 'Don't Start Crying Now', 'Baby Please Don't Go', 'Gloria' (1964) or 'Here Comes the Night' of March 1965 or the albums they released called simply *Them* (1965) and *Them Again* (1966).

The raw, almost belligerent energy of Morrison's voice spoke directly of and to a generation coming into its own during the early 1960s. But there was much more involved than brash display. In 'The Story of Them', written by Morrison, the narrative recounts a Belfast literally opening out, as 'Blues come rolling down Royal Avenue/Won't stop by the City Hall/Just a few steps away/You can look up at The Maritime Hotel'.

Morrison's searching elaboration of the syllables of his tale is mocked by the quizzing lead guitar as the emerging generation in the actual story stare back at the world with bristling self-preoccupation. 'The Story of Them' is a mini-epic sung to the laid-back rhythms of talking blues:

> When friends were friends and company was right
> We'd drink and talk and sing all through the night
> And morning came leisurely and bright.
> Down town we'd walk and passers-by
> would shudder with delight. Hmnn – Good times.

The languor of Morrison's voice is underscored by the band's consistently fugitive and disconsolate backing. The characteristic note is of a past that has slipped away: 'It was a gas'. The instant retake on the band's life on the stage of The Maritime tells a rhetorical story about defiance and disdain ('We don't care') which is dramatised through the inflections of Morrison's Belfast accent. As he plays with individual words like 'Look' and toys with occasional harmonica rushes, Morrison's voice evokes not only an imaginative terrain but one that is literally in the mind's eye, summoned by the names and sounds of places and things:

> Barred from pubs, clubs and dancing halls
> Made the scene at the Spanish Rooms on the Falls
> And then four pints of that scrumpy was enough to have you
> out of your mind, climbing up the walls, out of your mind.

Acknowledging the help of 'The Three Jays' – Jerry McKenna, Jerry McKervey and Jimmy Conlon, young promoters on the music scene in the early 1960s – Morrison laments, 'It was something else then'. With a surprising lack of sentimentality or nostalgia, questions are asked and answered in an impersonation of the audience's view of what they, the audience, are looking at on stage. 'The Story of Them' is Morrison in dramatic monologue:

> People say, 'Who are *Them*?' Or 'What are *Them*?'
> That little one sings and that big one plays the guitar
> With a thimble on his finger, runs it up and down the strings;
> Bass player don't say much:
> I think they are all a little bit touched.

The colloquial idiom of 'a little bit touched' runs alongside the self-consciousness of the whole number and the ambiguous, contradictory relationship between band and audience, time and place is summed up in the simple declaration:

> Wild, sweaty, crude, ugly and mad,
> Sometimes just a little bit sad.
> Yeah, they sneered and all,
> but up there we were just having a ball.
> We are *Them*, take it or leave it,
> Do you know they took it,
> And they kept coming.

Morrison departs the song, 'just a little bit sad/gonna walk for a while/wish it well'. A gesture which features in so many of his lyrics as the insider leaves with the knowledge that to return is always afterwards going to be qualified by the fact of leaving.

What is clear from the recordings of Morrison with Them is the self-belief and confidence in what they are doing on stage. As he says in 'The Story of Them', 'The people kept coming'. In The Maritime, and the other small clubs around Belfast, an audience was building up for the peculiar mix of blues, r & b and a folk-jazz reminiscent of Dylan. This growing audience, mainly young, working-class and lower-middle class, had previously been invisible. They were children of the welfare state and the first generation to really benefit from the steady if slow upswing in economic fortunes during the late 1950s and the early 1960s. According to the historian David Harkness, 'Material conditions improved for many in both communities in these years, and many began to move into new housing areas where religions intermingled and good neighbours were found amongst traditional foes'. Notwithstanding what Harkness also refers to as the 'ingrained unemployment problem' which afflicted the northern economy, the mid-1960s reflected, at least on the surface, an image of the provincial capital as vibrant and in touch with what was going on in the world.

Variously billed as Belfast's Jazz Club and Rhythm & Blues Club, the Maritime Hotel in College Square North was a Merchant Seaman's Hostel built, on the site of a former Royal Irish Constabulary station, in 1945 by the British Sailors Society.

Situated with its back ironically shunning two of the city's most famous institutions of education, the Royal Belfast Academical Institution ('Inst') and the College of Technology, and equidistant between the city-centre and the bottom of the Falls Road, the Club in 1964 was the focus for Queen's University students and the outward-going and confident working class young.

In this most work-orientated of cities, where status and prestige was intrinsically linked to one's 'steady' job and prospects, the students had an identity of their own. As they meet up with working-class kids in their late teens or early twenties, a brief cross-over took place which was to last during the mid-years of the 1960s in Belfast. In passing, it's true to say that as things were to develop, with the eruption of the Troubles in the late 60s and early 70s, the Maritime, alongside other 'clubs' such as Sammy Houston's in Great Victoria Street, provided a chance for kids of every religion and none to get together. Such thoughts would have been far from the minds of those at the time, however; all that mattered was the music. For many working-class kids, seeing students look like 'beatniks' would have had a greater effect on them than wondering about what church they went to. The experience must have been something of a liberation from the conventions of previous generations when 'going out' meant dressing 'proper'. For the general rule had been that once the dungarees, factory-overalls or shop-clothes were taken off, it was time to 'dress up'.

The men, older brothers and uncles, next-door neighbours, with their hair quiffed and immaculately cut; after-shaved; a thin bar of white handkerchief in the breast-pocket of the Burton's Italian suit, the required showing of cuff with the monogrammed links and gleaming chelsea boots; their girls in dresses and imitation furs or 'swagger coats' always carrying in their handbags the silver dagger-like back-combing comb to ensure the look. Men would also always carry a comb in their back pockets. A Friday or Saturday night was the chance to be part of a picture-show in which everyone who ventured out had style and became an actor. Belfast's city centre, with the light spilling out from the plate-glass shop-front windows and the perpetual flow of buses, was actually like a stage set for drama. And drama there was. Lovers met 'down town', had drinks, went to the pictures or to a classy ballroom.

There could be bloody and at time vicious fist-fights, and worse, for the macho, vain or vanquished in this most intensely proud and symbolic display of male proprieties. Women would sometimes imitate. There could be operatic rows between dates in shop-doorways or at street-corners and on buses. Indeed, to circumnavigate Belfast's city centre on a weekend was often an experience in itself. For it was to watch (but not too intently for fear of ending up involved!) the clash between the theatrical and the everyday. Working life confronted itself with time off and was exposed in turn to the dream world of entertainment, leisure and possibility. A world, it was commonly believed, which 'the students' perpetually inhabited.

With their long hair, wearing whatever came their way from duffle-coats to old school blazers, flared pants, old ex-army leather jackets, polo-necks, jeans, suede shoes and Norfolk coats the students defied (if only for a few years) the working ethos of the city. They were an unknown quantity and, in a sense, Queen's students of the time lived in a quarantined world. They had a fool's pardon when they ventured through the city centre and would have been treated with short shrift during the mid-1960s had they made their presence felt at the ballrooms and larger dancehalls whose audiences were, to a man and woman, working hard for the rest of the week. This was also true of some of the city bars.

It's hardly surprising, therefore, that the students would find their own venues such as the Maritime. From being a venue for variety-type concerts as well as trad jazz, The Maritime became synonymous with r'n'b, the music which symbolised a breaking away from, and loosening of, custom. On the ground floor a cafe faced up to a flight of stairs, and along the narrow institutional-like painted passageway, there was a small dance hall. It had a low stage and bands would often walk through the audience to reach the stage, or, having finished their set, simply jump down from the stage and mill about with the audience. They played short sets of half-an-hour to forty minutes, local band following local band, or sometimes a visiting band. Belfast was very much part of the British circuit and most of the well-known and not so well known bands of the time played the city. The Maritime had, however, enough of its own bands to turn over two or three each night. They looked like their audiences and did whatever they fancied on stage; smoking and drinking. The Maritime was breaking down the expected notion of musical entertainment as something which is 'provided by' an ensemble of musicians into something created between themselves *and* the audience.

No showband uniforms here nor spangling glacial mirrors. The formal paired dancing of the ballrooms, even the riskier jive, gave way, and at other similar clubs, to solo expression, body to body, which had a sexual frankness well beyond the sophisticated flirting and masquerade of showband music. No wonder I can recall the excitement of a friend's older sister telling us about this 'brilliant' dance-club and then demurring in front of her mother about whether or not it would be a fit place for boys 'our age'. So that by the time we had moved in to the Maritime, just after Them had broken up, and it had become better known as Club Rado, the name of the Maritime was associated with excitement and risk and a sense of being part of a generation.

It was in actual fact an extraordinarily confined space with people crammed everywhere. The r'n'b ethos was religiously maintained by bands such as Sam Mahood and the Just Five, the slightly more college-based blues of The Few whose patron saint was John Mayall, a regular visitor to the city with his Bluesbreakers, and the fervent Soul of The Interns. Later on Rory Gallagher and Taste played regularly at the Club.

Added to this 'tradition' of a few years' standing imported bands whose showmanship often superseded musical skills were eager to play at the Maritime. Arthur Brown's Experience, who arrived on stage with a headpiece on fire to sing 'Fire', comes to mind.

In April 1964, when Morrison and Them first played the Maritime, the atmosphere would have been significantly different because the band and audience were part of something that was new. The exhilaration of the music that Them played was substantially a part of rejecting the established 'pop' music of the time, particularly in Ireland. Dublin had 'pop' and 'soul' bands as indeed had Belfast. But Morrison's voice, Them's music, dress and mannerisms were guaranteed to satisfy a feeling for rebellious self-assertion: what *against* was left to one side. The aggression is caught in the sound of the music, even when the song is of love-lost, the regret is tinged with anger. Them played a style of r'n'b that was not only good to dance to but was also conscious of itself. Being a fan of Them, as listening to r'n'b, for a generation, was subtly identifying oneself: in Belfast of that time, it carried the aura of being anti-establishment, with the Maritime as the cavernous symbol.

The anthem of that identification was 'Gloria', the flipside of 'Baby Please Don't Go', Them's second single, released in England in November 1964. The band had been playing for barely eight months but had now a record in the British charts, and an appearance on the prestigious Independent Television's 'Ready Steady Go' programme. Confirmation of their status came with the decision to use 'Baby Please Don't Go' as the programme's title-music.

Albeit with critical hindsight, it is true to say that Morrison's writing for 'Gloria' had found a perfect pitch: an aggressive and physical lyric which moves, literally step-by-step, towards sexual encounter.

The almost martial drumming which Morrison breaks into with his story, 'Like to tell you 'bout my baby', is urgent in its portrait of a midnight world:

> She comes walking down my street,
> Won't you come to my house
> She knocks upon my door
> And then she comes to my room
> Then she makes me feel alright.

The subjective territory of the song is stressed very much in the possessive – 'my' street, 'my' house, 'my' door and 'my' room. The link between streetlife and inner sanctum is hypnotically cast as the girl's name is spelt out: G.L.O.R.I.A. Whatever about the speculations as to who 'Gloria' actually was (a fate which pursues many of Morrison's lyrics, most famously 'Madame George') the focus is on the man and not the woman. That is what the shouting is all about. It were as if the singer was actually on the street, calling.

The echoey, sparse sound of 'Gloria' may well be the first 'punk' record as some maintain. For Morrison is, after all, writing out of a vibrant local idiom which prizes brash, almost confrontational, frankness. This did indeed involve calling out names and provocatively drawling vowels, as much as a summons as celebration. In the back of the song, too, the skipping tune accompanying a street game is not too far away from the emphatic rhythms, but transformed by the band from kid's stuff into passion.

All the more important, therefore, to recall the tone of suburban ennui and middle-class complacency which sickens the young Gavin Burke in Brian Moore's *The Emperor of Ice*

Cream published in 1965. Set in Belfast of the 1940s, Moore's portrait of the city as 'this dull, dead town' has remained for over thirty years the cultural stereotype. In contrast, Sam Hanna Bell's *The Hollow Ball* (1961) tells a different story:

> They decided on a walk in the Botanic Gardens before going downtown. The sun dropping behind the Castlereagh Hills glittered on the pastel coats of the women, the starched collars of the respectable young men, the diamonté ornament in Maureen's fur collar. There was a tingle in the air that pierced their hands and turned their laughter to smoke. At the entrance to the new rose garden he caught her hand and they fled under the rustic arches, past the children and the dogs, past the gaping park attendant fumbling in his memory for a by-law that restrained young men and pretty girls from running in the winter sunlight, past the rude young men hooting at them from the shelter by the bandstand.

What Bell is hinting at here, and what his novel overall dramatises, is the up and down sides of life in Belfast. The important thing is that, according to Bell, there was an upside, in the first place! The parks, the evening sunlight, the sexual joy and innocence, the music and, even while shadowed by that authority figure of the 'park attendant', there is that pronounced lyrical feeling of *possibility*. This is where Morrison comes in, with a vision all of his own conveyed through the exuberance of his voice.

With the demise of *Them*, after a time touring in England and in the States, Morrison's lyrics become preoccupied with what looks like a contradiction. For as Morrison discovers a rich thematic seam in writing about the Belfast he had grown up in, at the very same time, living in Belfast was frustrating him. 'As far as ideas and stuff were concerned,' he told Richie York, 'America was the place for me. That's the way it worked out . . . For Belfast, my ideas were too far out.'

Leaving Belfast in 1967 for New York, the twenty-one year old Morrison displayed not only tremendous courage but a forthright belief in his own artistic vision. As he remarked in an interview in 1987: 'All I did from the time I was eighteen to twenty-seven was work. I worked my way from Belfast to New York and didn't even know I was there because it was work.'

Like Bob Dylan leaving Hibbing, Minnesota at the turn of the decade, Morrison was willing to use whatever he wanted, to make up his own tradition out of diverse musical influences and literally forge a different kind of music. An iconoclastic individualism which, even to this day, has caused problems. This conviction, let us not forget, had to be sustained in the teeth of perhaps the most savage of industries, the music industry. That confrontation, a battle for survival, and his temperamental and intellectual reading of the media and pop culture, from *MTV* to what he has called 'The Great Deception' which feeds off the music scene, is a key to understanding Morrison's lyrics.

'It all comes down to survival', Morrison is quoted as saying in an interview with *Rolling Stone* (1990), 'and you can't intellectualise survival, because either you survive or you don't. That's the way life goes, and I'm not going to intellectualise it, because that's only going to spoil it.'

In 1968, having behind him years of playing with several bands from the Javelins and Monarchs to Them, working throughout Ireland, Scotland and England, touring Germany, and America, Morrison made in *Astral Weeks* an imaginative repossession of his own past and the language and landscapes associated with it. Much has been made about this particular album of Morrison's; justly so. It is important, however, to remind ourselves that like any performer, Morrison inhabits the stage as much as his work exists as recordings. The changing venues, musical contexts and audience expectations place the live performance in the realm of theatre, with the band as cast. As Morrison said: 'An album is roughly forty minutes of music, that's all'. There is in Morrison's work the feeling that the lyric sound is more important than the written song. The voice dominates what is sung because language turns into music at certain points; the tongue, the throat, the making of sound is its own instrument as Morrison was later to imitate pipe-music as a mantra; an incantation that can suggest the inadequacy of communication to *mean* something.

There is, then, in *Astral Weeks* the sense of what the journalist Seán O Hagan accurately calls Morrison's 'stretching the bounds of vocal expression to the limit'. This spontaneous yet formally experimental desire was very much part of the Beat Generation of the Fifties and early Sixties. As already mentioned, Morrison came in contact with Jack Kerouac and Allen Ginsberg through his reading. The influence of Kerouac, along with Ginsberg and Gary Synder, was, as the Beat Generation historian, Anne Charters pointed out, central in linking poetry and jazz together in an attempted New Vision, tracking back to Blake and Walt Whitman and also into Rimbaud and D H Lawrence.

In Morrison's situation, however, the controlling principle of his music is underscored by an inherited suspicion of artistic looseness. Morrison's poetic free form has never been excess but access; a contest between passion and restraint. Unlike the Beat poets' critique of American consumer culture, there is not the faintest interest in identifying alternative political or social mores in Morrison's writing.

The eight tracks of *Astral Weeks*, recorded in two days in New York and released in the US in November 1968, present a reverie: a consistent personal dramatisation of mood, landscape, romantic longing and nostalgia for a lost Eden. *Astral Weeks* explores this earlier age of innocence, but the songs do so without sentimentalising the imagined past.

The world of rivers, gardens, railway lines, particular avenues, can be identified with Morrison's youth in east Belfast. The site of that past becomes emblematic, rather than turned into local colour. Indeed, throughout *Astral Weeks*, as with Morrison's later albums, the naming of streets, districts, regions, takes on an incantatory significance. The memory returns again and again to its first home as the alluring poetics of space, rather than the specific meaning of the place.

Astral Weeks is not the sudden breakthrough it has so often been described; Morrison was after all working on these, and similar songs in Belfast well before leaving for New York. More importantly, the main thrust of the songs remain close in theme and imagery to his earliest recorded work with Them: tracks such as 'Hey Girl', 'Philosophy' and particularly 'Friday's Child'. There is too the clear line that runs through his first recordings with Bert Berns for Bang Records, such as 'Joe Harper Saturday Morning' and 'The Back Room'.

The significant shift is in the musical treatment. It has moved away from the hard-edged, probing 'group' sound with which Them channeled, indeed challenged, Morrison's voice. Instead the voice is articulated alongside the softer-focused, accoutisically-led accompaniment. For the guitar (Jay Berliner), bass (Richard Davis), flute (John Payne), vibraphone (Warren Smith) and drumming of the Modern Jazz Quartet's Connie Kay, fuse into an orchestration of strings. What is produced is one continuous mood-poem. Morrison's guitar might introduce the songs of *Astral Weeks*, but the poetic intention in his controlling voice is clear from the beginning of the title-track, 'Astral Weeks':

> To be born again, to be born again,
> To be born again, in another world darlin'
> In another world.
> In another time.

The desire in the voice, a hymn to love's possibility, picked out by the light touches of flute, strings and guitar, is guarded throughout *Astral Weeks* by a darker bass note that reminds us of uncertainty and vulnerability:

> Ain't nothin' but a stranger in this world,
> I'm nothin' but a stranger in this world,
> I got a home on high,
> In another land so far away, so far away.

Before Morrison laughs at himself at the song's end.

The setting for *Astral Weeks* could not be simpler: two lovers, separated 'from the far side of the ocean', are joined together throughout these love songs. They walk through gardens and experience one another in a dream state. (An earlier, less coherent version of 'Beside You' depicts their encounter in explicitly physical terms, with the male figure dramatised in a much more forceful sense.)

While this untroubled world seems out of reach, the songs record the poet's own surroundings, with intriguing and sometimes obscure references:

> Little Jimmy's gone way out of the back street,
> Out of the window, to the fog and rain,
> Right on time, right on time.
> That's why Broken Arrow waved his finger down the road
> So dark and narrow,
> In the evening just before the Sunday six-bells chime,
> Six-bells-chime,
> And all the dogs are barking.

The city landscape is left behind as 'the country where the hillside mountains glide' comes into view and in this Chagall-like transfiguration, the two young lovers meet, 'in the silence easy':

> You turn around, you turn around, you turn around,
> You turn around, and I'm beside you, beside you.

These love songs are all about an uncomplicated joy and the sense of release that singing his love's praises brings, troubadour fashion, as in 'Sweet Thing':

> And I will raise my hand up into the night time sky,
> And count the stars that's shining in your eye,
> Just to dig it all and not to wonder, that's just fine,
> And I'll be satisfied not to read between the lines.

The childlike love these songs court is literally of another time. In one of the best-known lyrics from *Astral Weeks*, 'Cypress Avenue', Morrison reimagines the play between young lovers:

> You came walkin' down, in the wind and rain, darlin',
> When you came walkin' down, the sun shone through the trees
> And nobody can stop me from loving you baby,
> So young and bold,
> You're fourteen years old.

There is, though, a further element introduced in 'Cypress Avenue' as Morrison touches upon inarticulacy, that much-vaunted feature of Northern Irish cultural identity and one which Morrison has explored (and made sport of) in live performances. In this instance, though, the issue is romantic (almost illicit) love. The expressiveness fights against itself, notwithstanding the Presley quotation, and tells a story of how difficult it is to say things; to communicate powerful feelings:

> And my tongue gets tied
> Every, every, every time I try to speak
> And my insides shake just like a leaf on a tree.

What makes 'Cypress Avenue' such an important song in Morrison's writing as a whole is the version of home which pervades it.

Is that 'Mansion on the Hill', Stormont: barely a stone's throw from the actual Cypress Avenue? The railroad, that disused railroad which runs nearby Holywood, Bloomfield, Orangefield and Ballyhackamore? But what about those 'Six white horses on a carriage/Just returning from the Fair'? And what about that 'Yonder' – one of those words which co-exist with the vernacular, (as in 'Look at your man yonder') and with an archaic literariness. 'Cypress Avenue' *reads* like an old English lyric but *sounds* like a Belfast street-song. Between the formal poetry and the physical setting, Morrison's voice generates a troubled robust ending amidst 'the avenue of trees'.

In 'Cypress Avenue', and the other songs from *Astral Weeks* an imaginatively coherent image of Belfast emerges, particularly of course for those who grew up in the city.

The residential patterning of the parts of the city such as north and east Belfast revealed a scallop-shell of class segregation, not matched by other districts. Clustered around the lough on both shores, the working-class districts fanned out and upwards, via main arterial roads, spliced with boulevard avenues, and often embracing distinctive districts that had once been villages along with, in the 1950s and 60s, the new estates. The patterning incorporated rescheduled water-ways, rivers, streams as well as enclosed cemeteries, displaced big houses of once prosperous merchants, and maintained parks and green-sites before reaching hillsides such as Castlereagh.

As previously noted, this redbricked civic landscape of back-lanes, 'entries', streets, terraces, roads and avenues had a definite if rarely articulated class-formation. To move within it was to experience the all so visible distinctions of a provincial urban society. To move literally from it was to encounter the shifting magical thresholds between city and country. Morrison's songs are powerful testaments to both these levels of perception. The mysterious luminous quality of *Astral Weeks* is earthed in the wonder, surprise and customs associated with leaving his own back-bedroom, going down his own street ('as we said goodbye at your front door', he says in 'The Way Young Lovers Do') to inhabit his own district, its daylight and nightlight, walking through Beersbridge and Orangefield, taking in everything.

Cypress Avenue is not only a place, it was the idea of another place; the railway, the river: all are conduits through which Morrison's imagination is freed.

'Madame George', the key lyric in *Astral Weeks*, dramatises this condition with a haunting portrait of belonging and leaving. This lyric, with its story-telling and repetitions, the anarchic mantra of 'the love' it seeks to express and its almost obsessive questioning, suggests comparison with the poet Patrick Kavanagh.

It is pure coincidence of course that Kavanagh, who was in the States in 1965 for a symposium on W.B. Yeats, should remark that he (Kavanagh) was all in favour of the Beat poets. 'I like Corso, Ferlinghetti, and Allen Ginsberg very much . . . there are these lads in America, these youngsters that I admire very much.'

What Kavanagh saw in the work of the Beats is curious given the Irish situation he had in his mind. They had, he said, 'all written direct, personal statements, nothing involved, no, just statements about their position. That's all. They are not bores as far as I am concerned.' Kavanagh's voice of dissatisfaction with convention ('boredom'), strengthened by his subjective romanticism ('direct personal statements') is very close to the poetic vision of *Astral Weeks* and in particular to the voice which recites 'Madame George'.

I first heard the song early in 1969 from the US album somebody had got a copy of and by the time it was released in the UK in September of that year *Astral Weeks* had become cultic.

Memory plays tricks with historical reality but it seems to me looking back over twenty-five years towards the twelve months between the end of 1969 and 1970, that everyone was playing *Astral Weeks* throughout the Belfast which I knew.

That year was a watershed for every generation in Belfast but particularly so for those of us who were leaving our teenage years behind and becoming young men and women. Friends would soon go their own way, across the water to England, taking up jobs, going to college, disappearing. The months leading out of the Sixties into the Seventies correspond, loosely and in an inchoate and inarticulate way, with a social and cultural breakup of life as we had known it.

'Madame George' captured that feeling, and still does. It was a strange quiet before the storm. The clubs were still doing good trade, parties at weekends, visiting big names from Jimi Hendrix, Pink Floyd, The Small Faces played the Ulster, King's or Whitla Hall. People hung out and there was little aggro, except for the usual sort of fighting that made Belfast city-centre a dangerous place some Saturday nights. But you could still walk throughout the wider city without too much anxiety or fear. But within a matter of a year or so, you took your life in your hands for so doing.

'Madame George' gives that freer time a distinctive sound and context. The shock of hearing the phrase, 'On a train from Dublin up to Sandy Row' has never quite left me. An inexplicable connection, coded beneath the words themselves, identified for the first time the actual city in which I lived.

Sandy Row, a protestant working-class district in Belfast's inner-city through which the train runs, is named; the custom of throwing pennies into the Boyne River (the iconographic site for the protestant defence of the British Crown and Faith in Ireland) which we did without knowing why, and the transfixing 'trance':

> Sitting on a sofa playing games of chance,
> With your folded arms in history books you glance,
> Into the eyes of Madame George.

Much has been read into this extraordinary song. For me, it is an *aisling*, 'a child-like vision' which portrays a world of loss and gain, ceremonies and evasions, past and present, shifting like a carousel between real and imagined people and places.

The soldier boy who is 'older now with hat on, drinking wine'. How many streets and roads had a few such men, tripping home after the pubs closed, at odds with the world they returned to and the front rooms, 'filled with music/Laughing music, dancing music'?

'Madame George' is a portrait of a society about to withdraw from public view at the same time as the voice which describes it is also leaving the scene. Memories shift and coalesce. The site of the poem blurs and moves in and out of focus. It is the Belfast of Cypress Avenue; there is a Fitzroy Avenue too. The rituals of 'collecting bottle-tops/Going for cigarettes and matches in the shops' are identifiably Belfast. But the journey is on a train from Dublin up to Sandy Row; and there is a Fitzroy Avenue in Dublin. Parsing the song in this fashion does not take us far. What is constant is the voice and the connections which the accent makes between 'raps', 'cops', 'drops' and 'gots'.

The unmistakable, unique and lasting nature of Morrison's achievement, from the late '60s to the '90s, is the steady, unflinching challenge which first his voice and then subsequently his lyrics and music embodies. The voice is a powerful ambiguity, revelling in itself, but dismissive too, while the lyrics have explored (and anticipated) much of the imaginative ambition and desire of Morrison's poetic peers. Van Morrison's first major album, *Astral Weeks* appeared in 1968, the same year as Derek Mahon's first collection, *Night Crossing*. Clustered around that year too, one can identify a new and powerful generation of Irish poets emerging out of the post-war period: Seamus Heaney, *Death of a Naturalist* (1966), *Door into the Dark* (1969); Michael Longley, *No*

Continuing City (1969) with its 'Words for Jazz Perhaps' updating Yeats; James Simmons, *Late But in Earnest* (1967) and *In the Wilderness* (1969); fellow-east Belfastman Stewart Parker, *The Casualty's Meditation* (1966), *Maw* (1968) (and whose 'High Pop' column in *The Irish Times* hailed Morrison's albums with bright intelligence and insight); and, from the south of Ireland, the poet contemporary most close with Morrison in so many respects, Paul Durcan, whose first publication (shared with Brian Lynch who was subsequently to write a stage-play with the Morrison title, *Conquered in a Car-Seat*), *Endsville* (1967).

Like other Irish artists before him, Morrison's move to America was a liberating one at the time. The albums which followed *Astral Weeks* – *Moondance* (1970), *Tupelo Honey* (1971), *St. Dominic's Preview* (1972), *Hard Nose the Highway* (1973) are an imagining of America and the extraordinary sense of freedom (as well as obsessiveness) associated with the place. As the literary critic and cultural commentator, John Wilson Foster has remarked about his own upbringing in east Belfast during the 1940s and early '50s, 'We grew up steeped in American popular culture. America was the fourth country we lived in.'

The 'years of hope', as Jonathan Bardon accurately described the period 1945-1968, etched themselves ineradicably in the emotional, cultural and political experience of an entire generation. Morrison gives voice to both the hope and excitement, the energy and drive, shadowed by the knowledge of loss and pain. It is a fusion at the core of Stewart Parker's writing, as well; most emphatically, in his greatest play, *Pentecost*.

PART TWO

◆

A HARD ACT
Stewart Parker's Pentecost

I

In the mid-1960s Stewart Parker gave a class at Orangefield. The class he gave was on the poetry of Sylvia Plath and, afterwards, I spoke shyly to Stewart Parker and confessed that I wrote poems. His smile was encouragement enough to a fifteen-year-old. I have admired Stewart Parker from a distance, never having met him again; his death, at 47 in November 1988, robbed Irish literature of one of its most liberated and articulate voices.

From *Catchpenny Twist* produced in The Peacock in 1977, the idea of Parker's liberating creative intelligence struck me with even more force in *Northern Star* (The Lyric 1984) and, with the Field Day production of *Pentecost* in Derry, 1987, I realised that Parker was indeed a great playwright. Rough Magic's stunning production of *Pentecost* (1995) underscored this realisation with renewed conviction.

Pentecost is a contemporary classic play, as central to Irish experience as *Translations, Double Cross, Bailegangaire*, and *Observe the Sons of Ulster*. In what follows I'd like to illustrate why I think *Pentecost* is an important play. My conclusion points towards the cultural resistance and uncertainty which still exists in Ireland, and elsewhere, when writing, bearing upon northern protestant experience, is addressed.

Pentecost takes place in east Belfast (Ballyhackamore) during the Ulster Workers' Strike against the Sunningdale Agreement between British and Irish governments. The strike was in particular directed against the Council of Ireland dimension to that Agreement. The strike lasted from 14 to 29 May and was successful. It brought down the power-sharing Executive.

Pentecost begins in February 1974, moves into April, and focuses upon the two weeks between Sunday May 19, Saturday 25 and concludes on June 2. Pentecost (Acts: 2) is a religious convocation marked in Christian churches on the 7th Sunday after Easter, *Whit Sunday*.

Belfast in 1974 was a ghost town; the workers' strike turned it into a bizarre disconnected statelet. I was sitting my final exams that May and June and recall my father driving me through roadblocks from east Belfast, stopping to get petrol at which the UDA guy in a balaclava, carrying a stick, flagged us on, and wished me good luck in the exams.

'[T]housands of hooded men with clubs' as Parker has it in the play, but there was no widespread display of guns, contrary to conventional wisdom.

In the five years of the Troubles, by 1974, there were 1,000 dead, 620 of the victims in Belfast alone. Within the next year or so, 25,000 houses had been destroyed. In the first two weeks of May 1974, there had been 11 killings and 13 bombs had gone off. Sectarian warfare was engulfing Belfast: republican paramilitaries were destroying the civic life of the city with terrifying rigour. To go out and about, people literally took their lives in their hands. The loyalist response was nightly assassinations, bombing pubs and sacking streets. It is important to remember what the people of Belfast have actually gone through: caught in a historical trap not of their own making, their fate was to play out some undisclosable finale.

As W.A. Maguire remarks in his study of *Belfast* (1993):

> . . . in the first four years of the Troubles somewhere between 30,000 and 60,000 people in the Greater Belfast area were driven to leave their homes, at that date possibly the largest enforced movement of population in Europe since the Second World War.

Homes were burnt down; people were intimidated from their own houses and squatters moved in under the protection of one of the various defence committees. This is the backdrop to *Pentecost*. Precious wonder, then, that Parker referred to the play being written in a form of 'heightened realism' and certainly not 'the conventions of a broadly realistic piece' by which it has been described. Parker makes his intentions clear in the stage directions: 'Everything is real except the proportions. The rooms are narrow, but the walls climb up and disappear into the shadows above the stage'. The atmosphere of the entire play, inhabited as it is with ghosts and ghostly figures of dead and haunted men, lost children, ominous shouts, scuffles, helicopter searchlights, jegs of broken bottles on the yard wall, drumming – these all create a claustrophobic world that is surreal.

Moving through the five acts are five characters: two catholics – Lenny (to whom the house has been willed) and his estranged wife, Marian (who wants to buy the house); their two protestant friends – an old college pal, Peter Irwin who has returned to Belfast from Birmingham, and Ruth Macalester, the evangelical friend of Marian.

The shade of the sitting tenant, Lily Mathews, custodian of Belfast history ('1900-1974. This house was her whole life', Marian remarks) and in whose house the entire play takes place, enjoins a cast of unseen figures: Lily's own husband, Alfie, 'a good man'; Alan Ferris, the English airman and lodger, with whom Lily has had an all-too-brief affair, and a baby which she has given up, 'in the porch of a Baptist Church. [to] . . . moneyed people'; Ruth's demented RUC husband, who ends up in mental asylum after repeatedly beating Ruth and turning upon himself; and the little baby of Marian and Lenny, Christopher, who lived for five months.

The play is suffused with references to protestant churches, Sunday school, hymns (Lily's singing of 'Rock of Ages' ironically anticipates the victory hymn of the Workers' Council); gospel (Lenny playing 'Just a Closer Walk With Thee'); mythologised northern protestant experience of the First World War, the shipyard, the landscape and streetnames of east Belfast (Lily refers to her lover buying her a dress in 'Price's Window', a famous store on the Newtownards Road). There is also a depth-charged link, easily mislaid in hastily formulated interpretation, between the significance of the play's title and the reality-altering vision which pervades and ultimately transforms the character's lives:

Marian   Have you never considered that if one of us needs treatment it might be you?

Lenny   I never know how you do this, I start off trying to help you, and within ten minutes I'm a villain, I'm a deviant, I'm the one in need of help, in the name of God just face reality!

Marian   Which reality did you have in mind?

Lenny   Your own, Marian, your own reality, you've been talking to yourself, you've been counting spoons, you've been babbling in tongues in the middle of the night! . . . What are we supposed to think?

Marian   Don't think, Lenny. Don't think anything at all. Don't even try. It doesn't agree with you. Here's what we're doing. I'm staying here with my tongues – and you're going home with your trombone. That way we're all quits. Okay?

One of the most powerful elements in this marvellous play is the fact that Parker dramatically assimilates the apocalyptic, biblical vision (the babbling of tongues as the presence of the Holy Spirit) into the psychology of pain and loss which characterises the lives on stage, particularly the women's lives. He has also convincingly conceived women characters such as Marian and Lily, and less centrally, Ruth. While their childlessness becomes a subdued focus in the play, the dramatic metaphor of 'the house' as home and refuge becomes both moral and mystical shelter, as 'good' means 'washed', spotless, without blame;

Lily   Four of you's now, in on me, tramping your filth all over my good floors.

Within the house, Marian discovers Lily's diary as if it were a testament; while the christening gown of Lily's child, trimmed with lace and ribbons, merges naturally with the ceremonial white robes of Whit; and even Peter's awful bag of muesli can be seen half-seriously as a token of first-fruits. Be that as it may, the theatrical symbolism of this house is everywhere in the language of these broken characters. For 'house' read 'home-place', which means Belfast, Peter's 'Lilliput'; whatever tensions surface, they revolve around possession, of being 'at home'. Having fled violence in her own home, Ruth attacks Peter for losing touch with his own people:

Ruth   You don't know what's been happening here. What the people have gone through. How could you. You got out.

The moral weight of 'You got out' doesn't get in the way of Ruth and Peter making love, but it hangs over the play, like an indictment. Leaving or staying, homesick or sick of home, taking over a place or being evicted from it, the seesawing of the arguments between Ruth and Peter, Marian and Lenny – and which also include the infamous Harold Wilson broadcast, denouncing the unionist reaction as 'sponging on Westminster and British democracy' – all are based inside Lily's parlour house, 'eloquent with the history of this city', as Marian describes it.

It is a history which is class-conscious too, as Marian points out to her disenchanted trombone-playing husband: 'Well away you and explain all that to your Uncle Phelim [a psychiatrist], if you can track him down in his underground bunker, it's somewhere up Fortwilliam way, isn't that right?'

The catholic upper middle class retreated towards the upper reaches of the northern side of the city; previously such districts had been the reserve of predominantly wealthy protestant and Jewish communities. What ensues in this exchange between Lenny and Marian shows the extent to which Lily's house earths the dramatic force of *Pentecost*. Marian starts to sound like Lily, and, at the age of thirty-three, she is Lily's age when Lily was most alive. Addressing Lenny, Marian says:

Marian	I'm seeing this through. That's all. On my own terms. For Jesus' sake just leave me in peace, the whole shower of you, I'm sick of your filth and mess and noise and bickering, in every last corner of the house, I've had enough … You find a refuge, you find a task for your life, and then wholesale panic breaks out, and they all come crowding in the door, her [*Ruth*] and you [*Lenny*] and that trend-worshipping narcissist [*Peter*].
Lenny	It's beside the point, you're in terrible danger, we've all got to get out of here. The last thing I ever intended or needed, me and you under the same roof, it was another one of his lame jokes (*Gesturing skywards*) okay, we move out, we go our separate ways to our respective families. I don't like to see you in the state you're in. You're just not fit to be left on your own.
	(*Marian slowly turns on him*)
Marian	What are you getting at?

Lenny	I'm talking about what's going on!
Marian	Such as?
Lenny	What have we been having this entire conversation about?
Marian	You consider that I'm cracking up?
Lenny	When did I say that?
Marian	Not fit to be alone?
Lenny	In this house, that's all!

The talk is all about the place, at-homeness: 'in every last corner of the house', 'refuge', 'door', 'roof' etc. Throughout *Pentecost* the notion of belonging and of sustaining relationships with one another and to one place ramifies with similar terms of reference. But it is no longer 'just' the house; it is with living and being; or to use that desperate old Cold War jargon, 'co-existing': man and woman, protestant and catholic, the living and the dead; past and present. The history of this possibility – of redemption, self-belief, common bonds, sharing – is clearly established in the third act of *Pentecost*. Peter and Lenny are talking in superficial, blunt male terms about Marian:

Lenny	It's the state she's in . . . totally obsessive, don't ask me what the story is . . . some weird syndrome, you know how it is with women. I'm just thankful she's finally agreed to a divorce.
Peter	Would it still be losing the kid, maybe?
Lenny	That? – oh, she took that in her stride ... didn't she ... no problem. Anyhow. It's five years now.
Peter	Can't be.
Lenny	Near as dammit. August '69.
Peter	A Vintage month.

August 1969 remains the watershed in many northern minds, particularly for those in their late teens and twenties living in the city, jockeying back and forth to London, caught up in the music of the time. It was the symbolic breakpoint, because after that date the north entered the nightmare; beforehand, it felt like an indian summer of endless parties and clubland. In a sense, *Pentecost* is a hymn to the self-consciousness of that lost time. Written as part of a triptych of history plays in the mid-1980s when the cycle of violence seemed unbreakable, Parker found in *Pentecost* a form for exorcising what he called the playwright's 'gift or sentence' which is 'to function as a medium, half-hidden in the darkness, subject to possession by the ghosts of other voices, often truer than his own'.

What formed Parker's own voice is neatly summed up by himself in a bright and witty piece he wrote on James Joyce called 'Me & Jim'. Coincidentally, it is a list of priorities which neatly contextualises the themes of *Pentecost*:

> My own mind was framed by an urban neighbourhood, a working-class family struggle towards petit-bourgeois values, a recoil from home and church and country, an appetite for exile.

I may be deluding myself but the voice of Stewart Parker which I hear has a faint American inflection and the style of the man links him immediately with my own vintage. Through the 25 years of the Troubles, the sanity and wit and guile of Parker's plays logged the dismay, devilment and anguish of a generation which couldn't believe that what was taking place in its home was actually happening.

The belief and conviction that we were all one, irrespective of religion, if not of politics, was shattered. That sectarian violence and the lurid respect and support it received from so many, often distant sources, had become a sickening reality which was poisoning every hope and expectation.

Pentecost plays out this tragi-comedy with a series of stories that are neither ponderous nor self-considering. In the powerful, concluding moments of the play, Parker captures the crazy contradictory energy of his characters and the cultural world they know inside and out.

Marian   I'm clearing most of this out. Keeping just the basics. Fixing it up. What this house needs most is air and light.

And as they tell one another stories – Marian and Lily's night of passion; Lenny recalling seeing 'a gaggle of nuns, real nuns, stripping off' and swimming, 'experiencing their sex'; before Ruth reproves him for not understanding what 'Christianity' is about:

Ruth	You don't even know what day it is now, the meaning of it.
Peter	You tell them, Ruthie child. Pentecost Sunday.
Lenny	So what?

What follows is an extraordinary moment in Irish theatre and probably one of the most misunderstood scenes as well. It has been called 'a cop out' and 'dramatically problematic' and clearly caused unease. In my estimation the misunderstanding has got much more to do with cultural difference than many in Ireland and Britain are prepared to acknowledge.

As the stories interweave, Ruth and Peter recite between them 'The day our Lord's apostles were inspired by the Holy Spirit', to which Marian responds by talking about Christopher, the child she has lost. The scene, in what Elmer Andrews has called Parker's 'self-conscious theatricality', runs a great risk of falling like O'Casey into pathos, but the energetic and disciplined performances of both Eileen Pollock (in the original Field Day production) and Eleanor Methven (in the Rough Magic production) maintained the religious rhetoric with a strict and passionate delivery:

Marian	Personally, I want to live now. I want this house to live. We have committed sacrilege enough on life, in this place, in these times. We don't just owe it to ourselves, we owe it to our dead too . . . our innocent dead. They're not our masters, they're our creditors, for the life they never knew. We owe them at least that – the fullest life for which they could ever have hoped, we carry those ghosts within us, to betray those hopes is the real sin against the christ, and I for one cannot commit it one day longer.

I cannot think of a finer tribute of commemoration than this. Unlike other critics, I do not read the scene as 'a self-conscious break with naturalism'; because I do not see the play in terms of the usual conventions of naturalism, in the first place. It strikes me that this speech and Ruth's opening her Bible and reading aloud of the second chapter of Acts is a metaphorical resolution completely in keeping with the 'heightened realism' of *Pentecost*. Critics are uncomfortable with the tone, but target the style instead. 'Thou hast made known to me the ways of life; thou shalt make me full of joy with thy countenance' leads into Lenny's playing 'a very slow and soulful version of 'Just a Closer Walk with Thee' before Ruth opens the window, echoing Marian's earlier comment about what the house 'needs most is air and light'.

The ethos of *Pentecost*, taking into account its fun and laughter, and the caustic wit that sparks off between the couples, challenges certain kinds of (almost) subconscious critical categories, both in the Republic of Ireland and to a lesser extent in Britain. While *Pentecost*, particularly through Peter, condemns the lack of political generosity within the 'so-called protestants' yet the underlying picture defies easy notions of cultural stereotyping. The play takes Lily as its defining point of reference and dramatically explores the complexity, limitations and connectedness of protestant culture within Northern Irish society. It takes that society as *culture*, not solely as *prejudice*.

Parker was well aware of what he was doing and in the Introduction to his *Three Plays for Ireland* (1989) he remarked:

> The ancestral wraiths at my elbow are (amongst other things) Scots-Irish, Northern English, immigrant Huguenot . . . in short the usual Belfast mongrel crew, who have contrived between them to entangle me in the whole subject for drama which is comprised of multiplying dualities: two islands (the 'British Isles'), two Irelands, two Ulsters, two men fighting over a field.

Many writers and critics of Irish writing have problems with this reality and ignore it or wish-fulfil it away. Indeed, its critical invisibility is worth nothing. For instance, in the most impressive and sweeping historical survey to date on literature and drama in Ireland, Declan Kiberd's *Inventing Ireland: The Literature of the Modern Nation* (1995), Stewart Parker's name does not appear once, not even in a passing reference. Yet I cannot think offhand of another playwright who, in the space of roughly a decade between the mid-1970s to the late 1980s, offered more light *specifically* on the various historical Irelands which inhabit the country called the Ireland.

Parker was nothing if not switched-on to the here-and-now, the present, whether that be in his charade of *Catchpenny Twist*, or the poignant insights of the television play *I'm a Dreamer, Montreal*, or in the three plays which he saw as forming one historical meditation, 'a common enterprise' as he called it, closing with *Pentecost*.

As Parker said in his *John Malone Memorial Lecture*, 'Dramatis Personae' (June 1986):

> New forms are needed, forms of inclusiveness. The drama constantly demands that we re-invent it, that we transform it with new ways of showing, to cater adequately to the unique plight in which we find ourselves. For those of us who find ourselves writing from within a life-experience of this place, at this time, the demands could not be more formidable or more momentous.

Forms of inclusiveness? I think we have still a long way to go in being able to live up to Stewart Parker's comment about *Pentecost* when he spoke 'for my own generation, finally making its own scruffy way onto the stage of history and from thence into the future tense'.

PART THREE

◆

THE REST IS HISTORY
Belfast Notes
(1984–1993)

I

The four lads at the back of the bus were talking. And then the rip of a metal tab as another can of Harp was opened.

'The only fuckin' thing is Pernod and lime.'
'Na. Harp and cider.'
'He's a scar from thar to thar, the size of a fist.'

My four and a half year-old daughter and I looked out the window. This was the last leg of a long, tedious bus journey to Belfast and the sun had come out splendidly. We were both tired and the conversation behind us grated on obsessively. They seemed so enclosed by their own world, violence at every turn of phrase, but when a Christian Endeavour student tried to engage them in talk, one of the lads offered her a swig of lager which she refused and fell silent. I thought she gave up very easily for an evangelist-in-the-making.

Every time I go home it feels that I am inhabiting two worlds, two time-scales and that they are running parallel to one another. The walk from Glengall Street, now with my daughter and a few bags in hand, and the rush across Great Victoria Street, takes me by the site of Sammy Huston's Jazz Club: *Frankie Connolly & the Styx, Sam Mahood & the Just Five, The Few* and all those great bands that visited there in the '60s and early '70s.

Twenty years ago: but I still find it difficult to write of that time or to reassemble in my mind my feelings and expectations, because as one of a group from widely differing backgrounds the dangers did not seem so real. We grew away from Belfast, too, towards the allure of London and never thought that Belfast would succumb to 'The Troubles' like something out of Camus' *The Plague*.

We were, or some of us were, part of 'The Troubles', of course. It was important for us to understand what was going on – the marches, the political demands – but nothing, simply nothing, prepared us for the reaction either in terms of the mounting sectarianism – which we regularly had to circumvent – or the reality of the bombing.

When that came, effectively in 1970, our own lives took on a new weird meaning – we began to live more recklessly, with a perverse bravado, contemptuous of our backgrounds, we were like conspirators unconsciously losing contact with the usual ambitions and objectives of young men and women in their late teens and early twenties in an environment which was collapsing under its own weight. As Philip Larkin remarked in another context, 'At an age when self-importance would have been normal, events cut us ruthlessly down to size.'

The contingency of living with and thinking about such hostilities encroached with ever-steadier tread in the mid-'70s, by which time a few of the group had been through university or art-school and most had left the north.

But the year that stands out in my mind is 1974. Returning to live in Belfast from university at Coleraine, I started to work as a librarian in the Central Library. I hadn't really given the future, my own included, much thought, and work as a librarian seemed to be ideal. Maybe after experiences such as picking a child out of a bomb-blasted shop, having friends threatened, one killed, and watching corners of the city steadily disintegrate into rubble, the time was impractical and inauspicious. Whichever way I look at it, I know that that year of 1974 was the eye of the storm. I can even point to a particular scene when all this became clear to me.

One lunch time, I recall going down through the cool airy stairway of the library, becoming aware of a certain excitement at the swing doors which opened out on to the street. Making my way through a group gathered outside the library, between two bus stops and the red telephone kiosk, I eventually stood and listened to the clear intonations of an army officer informing the large crowd on both sides of the street that a bomb had been planted in a tailor's shop up the road from us. I knew the building well. It led round to Smithfield Market.

We stood, almost humbly, on our lunch hour, waiting, perhaps silenced, under instructions, irrespective of political leanings, religious inclinations, loyalties or whatever, depersonalised like a group of prisoners until finally the bomb exploded, a mass of shattering glass spilling on the ground, sundered brick sliding across the street to the squeals of women. Hesitantly at first, and then with more fluency, we went our separate ways. But just as the bomb went off, momentarily caught in the waves that plumbed the street, I saw a care-worn oldish woman, dressed in the usual sturdy, frayed overcoat and the workaday handbag, suddenly wince as if drowning in the sound of the explosion. Torn by its invisible pressure, she turned in a gasp into an image like that in Munch's *The Scream*. I grasped then how oppression works its way right through our very bodies and buries in our souls a physical terror that debilitates and makes acceptable the imposition of any final order. I think I also saw the deadly statis of history captured in the Englishman's poised language, in the blind gesture of violence and the ordinary drama of silently 'getting by' in our citizens' trail of survival.

It's really as if you had the choice of walking on two kinds of stairway – one fast, the other slower. Parallel stairways: this one is the present, the quick lane, of getting around the City Hall to a bus or taxi; the other, slowed to a measured pace, is the past. It's as if, thrown upon an imaginary screen, you can see yourself, going places, doing things, enlarged and selective. Nor is the experience necessarily unpleasant, but rather unsettling. It makes your present actions and thoughts seem transparent, as you look through them to see the past and how much (or how little) has changed. It forces you to focus more often on what is really there, until you get into the way of this double-take:

> *The Patriotic* turns to face
> an invisible sea. From Castle Place
> thousands swarm through side-streets
> and along the unprotected quays just
> to glimpse Carson, gaunt as usual,
> who watches the surge of people call,
> 'Don't leave us. You mustn't leave us',
> and in the searchlight's beam,

his figure arched across the upper deck,
he shouts he will come back
and, if necessary, fight this time.

The taxi-man had a black plastic refuse bag in the back
and said he was on his way to the dump when I hailed him.
Where to? I told him and off we went, bouncing around, the
faces of welcome at the familiar door as the taxi pulled up.

The week went quickly. I gave a few readings in schools;
my own first, at Orangefield, in the staffroom this time,
supping coffee and working out old days and old 'pupils',
walking along the same corridors and looking over the playing
fields to the Braniel estate. I was still thinking, though, of the
silent students I had just left, as they listened to this man
talking about their school and the people he knew when he
was there, about writing poetry and reading some:

You staged the ultimate coup de grâce
for the Union's son turned republican.
I can see you shivering in the cold
of an East Belfast morning, outside
school, the bikes upended, the quad
blown by a dusty wind, the rows of
windows, some cellophaned, gaze
back at the encroaching estate.

Next, over to Rupert Stanley College, sequestered in the
East End, with the fabulous crane 'Goliath', like a vast arch of
entry into the city. Then Sullivan Upper on the lough side,
where an oil-tanker edged out on the sea and a plane tipped
up into the sky, leaving the coastline in slow motion:

Deck-chairs gape at the sun
slinking down behind this part
of the Irish Sea. Between us
and the next landfall, trawlers
criss-cross shipping lines
fetching mackerel to protestant
villages along the shore.

On the bus back we had just a few on board, returning to
Portadown, Armagh, or Monaghan, *via* a route of small
villages all spruced-up and deserted on Sunday. The four

young hard nuts weren't to be seen. The following week, they
would be firing bricks at visored RUC men and giving camera-
crews the fingers. I sat staring out the window and wondered
what stairway *they* were on and how long they could stick it
before they would feel that break in time, fastened for a
second, as if the imaginary reel had broken down:

> On the hill
> in front of us
> the houses stretch up
> like a ladder from
> the Shore to Antrim Road.
> In-between is where we are,
> backs to the sea.

II

It was a choice between Art History in England or English in
Northern Ireland. Queen's in Belfast was too much like home
and when a friend said he was going to the New University of
Ulster, that was it. We headed off from Belfast one September
morning in 1971 and moved into the same B&B for the first
term. The house was run by a businesslike woman who took
good care of us and her house. Everything was in its place, put
there with a kind of brisk love.

Going to university was not the logical thing to do. Most
of my friends either had not bothered or did not get the
chance. We were, after all, children of the '60s, full of grace,
and it took some time to settle into the failed world that the
'70s brought. For some of us, it meant a struggle; for others, it
felt like a defeat. Anyway, Coleraine in 1971 was a
compromise. The campus looked like an airport but, behind
it, the Bann curved its way towards the coast and the
magnificent sea – along the shoreline where holiday resorts
clung, full of three– and four-storeyed guest houses with great
bay windows like puffed-out bellies – and a wind that would
cut right through you.

It was not long before a few of us – mostly from Glasgow and Belfast – had banded together and joined the Labour Club. NUU's political birth had been uppermost in many minds but, accepting the fact it was there to stay, we sat in seminar rooms and discussed the 'Law of the Diminishing Returns' and held a radical stall outside the refectory every week. When things were looking bad, some of us formed the 'James Larkin Defence Committee' and planned to get threatened catholics out of isolated places into safety. And we went on marches, to meetings and watched steadfastly as everything went from bad to worse. But we lived in a triangle that was symbolic in a way – between Coleraine, Portstewart and Portrush, the lines of communication were open and you could live freely, if experimentally, across the divides. Politics grew into Irish culture and back again into literature. We mixed into traditional music and some of the traditional musicians mixed into politics. I started to play in a band called 'Fir Uladh' and we performed at various venues, from anti-internment rallies to folk concerts. It was blissful. And, because I had written some poems which were published and broadcast, the Irish Dramatic Society asked me for a play. I wrote one – a short incoherent thing, the idea of which I had lifted from Robin Flower's *The Irish Tradition* – and called it *The Skull*. It was duly translated into Irish and, travelling with it, I was proudly introduced once as 'Our Belfast Protestant' to a smiling group of anxious Dublin Gaelgóirs.

We shared a year or two of confusion, living within that strange triangle. The people who lived there were mostly hospitable to these students in their midst. Even though our lifestyle was, on the face of it, a challenge to their own, I never heard a bad word said against us and only once in Coleraine did I hear 'the bigot' come out in a person. He was drunk and on his way home from the bar. The group of us, from all over the north, Scotland and England, and from every 'side', gazed at his ignorance and smiled sagely that his was an ugly old world shuffling off its mortal coil.

The three years did not last long. They were intense though. Everything was – sitting in the campus listening to the news of the Abercorn bomb blast, watching the slow dismantling of Belfast and the places we used to meet in back home. We threw darts in the university bar, while the literary critic and novelist Walter Allen held court, sipping pink gins and smoking his endless stream of untipped cigarettes; ensconced in the Anchor Bar, nestling beneath the convent in Portstewart, there was an air of unreality about the whole time and place.

The people of 'The Triangle', however, lived their lives with a keen knowledge we did not have. They were wise before the event and had an almost stoical single-mindedness about what was happening around them, as if it were a bad season they just had to thole. And us? The lectures went on as usual for those who cared to attend.

I remember, for instance, in one linguistics class, the distinguished lecturer, noted for his abstract convoluted manner and celestial gaze, talking us through the derivation of Cornish place-names. Three ex-Oxfordians sat midway up the lecture hall rigged-out as Red Indians with war paint and head-dress as a bet to show how oblivious the lecturer was of what was going on before him!

Such frivolity disappeared with time. The atmosphere became more obsessive, nervous, shaky. We held together, a generation at sea, but slowly being roped back in by the past. Some returned home to discover brothers had been lifted by the police, badly beaten, interned; or a man down the road was murdered, or another Provo bomb had scorched the life out of this street or that, and the inevitable retaliation. Everyday was becoming an aftermath of the wreckage from the night before.

The people grew suspicious, distant and hardened. Resentment spiked conversations. Still, we walked the coastline, travelling further north, west and south, discovering 'Ireland' and, finally, rented a fine house overlooking the Atlantic. My last year was spent there mostly – the white surf from the sea staining the windows, the damp of that big bedroom with its awkward wardrobes and the endless talk gripped by anger, uncertainty and the curse of everything that looked like going wrong.

The previous summer had shown us how fragile life actually was. Two of us were going to work June, July and August in the north of Scotland, building, of all things, an oil rig. We called down to Coleraine to book our flights and, wandering back to the little stations, I could smell something acrid burning. In split seconds, a bomb exploded some way behind us. People came slowly walking towards us, bewildered looks on their faces, calling to other people in doorways and all the while streaming by us. They just kept coming and we called out to stay back, pointing at a solitary car in the road. But they kept coming and we turned into the railway station, stunned a little, disbelieving. In the train, there was just the two of us so, when the second bomb went up, it felt like somebody had shouted out in the eerie silence of the carriage. We gaped at each other as the train pulled out. 'Jesus Christ,' Joe said, 'let's get the fuck out of here.' Within a year, we had all left that part of the country.

Of course, three years does not necessarily tell you much about a place. The triangle within which NUU shelters retains its wonder for me because of all that happened there. But sifting through those years, I recall a craggy bit of the coast down below the High Road when all you could see was the white spume of a turbulent sea and a rake of gulls, thrown up in the wind, screeching to their hearts' content. There was something exhilarating and disquieting about it – the dilapidated hotel with its broken windows and curtains flying out of them; all those tall houses closed in on themselves, as if the people were hiding. Maybe they were. Maybe we all were.

Then, in 1974, I went to Galway on the west coast of Ireland. My sense of the Belfast I had left is of a confused summer that included doing final university exams during the Ulster Workers' Council strike, juking through UDA barricades; several months working in the Central Library and moving across the deserted city at night to the small flat I had in Ballybeen estate. Then came a letter one morning offering me an award to write a thesis on the 19th-century Tyrone novelist and story-teller, William Carleton. So I worked my notice and inside a month travelled to Galway.

Standing in Eyre Square that first day in Galway, I felt wayward and discontented. I had been in the city once before, earlier that year, with a second play I had written for the Irish Language Dramatic Society, called *The Pawnbroker*. The occasion seemed so different now and, in the middle of this quick change of fortune, I was beleaguered and irresolute. The city, small and compact, is broken by many canals and bridges with high stone houses and warehouses which, in those pre-tax incentive development days, were roofless and windowless. Like all ruins, they had a poetic austerity about them. Walking around then, I felt a bit like a refugee but the main thing I wanted to do was fit in and be as inconspicuous as possible.

Nobody, of course, cared where I was from, but the thought ('Belfast and a protestant too!') weighed heavily with me and in the early days, trying to find a flat, some people were rather cool about renting to a gaunt-looking, intense young man who spoke too fast in a brash, emphatic accent. That first year I remember the perplexed outburst levelled at me: 'You've brought the Troubles with you!' Clearly, I must have assumed the same amount of interest on others' behalf as I was experiencing. It did not take long before I was, in some manner of speaking, in the swing of things. I frequented the Castle Hotel (now gone), where the Aran men assembled and some people from college. Or in the old Tavern where I recall Tony, the barman, opening, at my request, a hold-all that had been casually left it the foyer. It was the obvious things which took time to get over.

The impression I carried with me, like so many from a northern city background, that the 'south' was 'real country' – quaint, backward-looking and nostalgic – only highlighted my own ignorance and showed the extent of stereotyping that one absorbs. Galway was indeed dynamic, and full of all the cultural uncertainties, vitalities and differences one gets in any modern city or town. Underlying that, there was, too, a definite change of rhythm, a complicated difference of feeling. Not simply to do with *clichés* like closeness to nature, or the physical beauty of the landscape, the differences I discovered were part of the actual fibre of living in Galway: an emotional openness, an ease that seems to the outsider like complacency and a fierce instinct to keep going no matter what the odds. These are characteristics of people anywhere but, in the historical confluence of the west that I came to know, they struck me then as the most intriguing.

So too, by contrast, the 'types' I had grown used to from home were not around: the boozy clerks, the silver-rinsed spinsters, the hard-men – that self-enclosed northern earnestness and bravado was a world away from this place. Here people seemed to talk about foreign places, fishing, horses, language and history with a kind of confidence I had not met before so widespread and uncontrived. It took some time to overcome my rankling prejudice that this was all pretence, a surface gloss emulating the great Elsewhere.

There were, of course, little things that nagged away and proved irritating. For instance, the shifting diffidence to those who have 'done well' (meaning 'made money') and live in preposterous mansions on the outskirts of towns. Maybe the democratic spirit of the north is, ironically, of a more substantial kind than that of the south, whatever about the established rule and the order of the north's history of injustice.

One is naturally a magnet for like-minded people but most of those I came to know and whom I count as friends are from many different walks of life. I have noticed how their beliefs and prejudices have little of the introversion that so taints life in the north. They have seen through England but know it better and in a more complex way than many a die-hard Unionist, while their experience of living at the end of this century in a small and nominally independent country leads them to deal with the economic and social realities of *today* rather than with the cultural ideals of the last century. If their sympathy for what is happening to the north is blunted by disgust, their patriotism is similarly gagged by violence done in (and against) their name.

I have not gone to the Aran Islands – it is one of the several pilgrimages I have yet to make, like those to Clonmacnoise and the Ring of Kerry. The political past of the Republic is part of my family now. I am a citizen of sorts. As for the public show of its religion we hear so much about, it really is no more obvious and oppressive than all the innumerable churches, gospel halls, evangelical tents, monuments and epitaphs that dot the northern landscape. If such is how people believe, I see no point in condemning them left, right and centre because it isn't otherwise.

One night, after giving a poetry reading in Gort, Co Galway, a town full of literary resonances, I watched a bunch of kids pump pinball machines in one of those anonymous hamburger joints. It was a cool, damp evening without a cloud in the sky. The sound of a rock-band blared out the door. A police car patrolled down the square high above which stood a statue of Christ the King. Most of the other shops and houses of the main street were shut and dark. Behind them the countryside stretched away out, crossed by a railway track, small farms and various clumps of forest, forgotten old houses and endless lanes leading somewhere. For some reason, that night made me think of how the time had flown since I arrived here first, like any stranger, asking for directions.

III

One morning in 1965 I was sitting on the 64 Downview Bus, heading into town for school. It was raining and the bus was packed with people, most of whom were smoking cigarettes and looking out the steamed up windows. A strange thing happened. I looked around me and, in a flash of histrionic insight, realised, almost smugly, that they would, we all would, someday die. No proverbs; no sandwich men; no ministers; no amount of praying, church-going or piety could get us around that simple fact of life.

A few years later, I read until I was almost blue in the face everything by Jean-Paul Sartre and Albert Camus and considered that my earlier experience had been what every good existentialist knows to be an encounter with the Absurd. If Roquentin, Meursault and Mathieu were not exactly the best role-models for a Belfast protestant teenager, with a paltry attendance at Sunday school and church, who was supposed to know any the different?

The irony is, I suppose, that the family I came from, while not being orthodox in their religion – anything but – did have a lot of time for spiritualism. Life-after-death was a fairly acceptable norm. Not things that go bump in the night, hovering tables and trumpets of ectoplasm like a week's washing – although there was one book with photographs of such things that had a faintly Faustian sense of transgression about it, and still has to this day . . . No, the spiritual dimension to my upbringing ran quietly but constitutionally contrary to the eye-balling of existence that Sartre insisted upon. But, like a dutiful disciple, I was hooked by his militant agnosticism.

Roquentin remarks in *Nausea* – Penguin Modern Classics, June 1969, four shillings, Dali's *Triangular Hour* on the cover:

> Most of the time, because of their failure to fasten on to words, my thoughts remain misty and nebulous. They assume vague, amusing shapes and are then swallowed up. I promptly forget them.

And the rallying call I underlined clearly held no truck at all with religion, spirituality or the likes of that.

> I want no secrets, no spiritual condition, nothing ineffable; I am neither a virgin nor a priest, to play at having an inner life.

Why an 'inner life' should have been seen then as an almost derisory thing I cannot now recall. Yet, the 20-odd years which separate the underliner of that passage from the present writer has also seen, in Ireland as elsewhere, a great emphasis being put upon the confession publicly of one's innermost secrets and personal experience. The more beans of self spilled on stage, in print and on TV, the more honest, sincere, genuine, moving, powerful and realistic we are seen to be. Also, the more *artistic*. Spirituality is the goodly handmaiden; religion the ugly sister – or Christian brother – who beats the lard out of our natural state of innocence and well-being.

In rejecting all this tosh, the Duchamp portrait by Jacques Villon on the Penguin cover of *The Outsider* says it all. Angular, haunting, uncompromising and spooky, it embodies a feeling of calm, benign, hard-won indifference. Resisting sham solution, self-indulgence, fashionable anger, privileged resentments and preoccupied instead with austere moderation and artistic reserve, it should come as no surprise that Camus offered an alternative, if allied, vision to that generally on offer in post-war pre-Troubles Belfast.

It is something which Derek Mahon captures in his fine poem, dedicated to Camus, 'Death and the Sun':

> The interior dialogue of flesh and stone,
> His life and death a work of art
> Conceived in the silence of the heart.

What this might sum up is that existentialism was an aggressive way of bringing oneself up in a city coming down with passionless religion and atrophied politics. It was a thing of the heart; iron in the soul.

> On everything I love, on the rust in the yards, on the rotten planks of the fence, a miserly, sensible light is falling, like the look you give, after a sleepless night, at the decisions you made enthusiastically the day before, at the pages you wrote straight off without a single correction.

What Roquentin writes in his Diary was the real thing.

Where the spiritualism came in is something else altogether – a joker in the pack, the hazel wand that bewitches and divines truth rather than discerning the reality of a situation. This belief in an afterlife had a strong, palpable existence in the north of my childhood.

It is also something without which the suffering of the last twenty years in the north would have been even more unbearable for the hundreds of thousands of victims there. The testimony of so many in front rooms talking of their murdered loved ones before the cameras for the first time, bespeaks a faith in God, in an after-life, that cannot simply be smiled upon with condescension. Remove it and what is there to take its place?

So, I am less sure about religion and how it has stanched many wounds, ritualised and dignified what is so grim in its very ordinariness – death. If institutionalised religion has lacked sunlight, that probably tells us more about the north as a whole than it does about its churches and those who go to them. As Mahon's poem says:

> The modes of pain and pleasure,
> These were the things to treasure
> When times changed and your kind broke camp.

Times are changing. *Rigor mortis*, not rigour, is setting in with those who remain glumly satisfied with their own religious or political self-consciousness. But if pleasure comes from God, a church-bench, a meeting hall, or a marquee tent, who is to decree: *No, that's wrong?* It is, isn't it, a matter for the individual's free will and conscience? We risk this precise and exacting inheritance in the clamour to prove who we are and who is like us.

Yet, the place of literature has, until very recently, only been on the leafy margins of Belfast life. For instance, where we lived in north Belfast there were no writers, so far as I knew. One painter, an elocution teacher and piano-instructress, but no writers. Then, one morning I saw a man in a very dapper trench coat with a large briefcase standing in the bus queue and recognised his face from a photograph in *The Belfast Telegraph*. My mother confirmed the rumour that he was a writer – of novels – and lived in a flat just up from our house. He kept to himself and I have heard nothing about him since, although his novels were very well received when they were first published in the 1960s. Not that I knew that then, of course. I did not read Irish writers. I was brought up on Keats and Shakespeare at school and on an extraordinary mix of elocution anthologies at home, like the infamous *Palgrave* and lesser known *Albatross* in which my grandmother had ear-marked poems for recital. Stevenson's *Treasure Island* was the first book I really knew:

> Oxen and wain-ropes would not bring me back again to that accursed island; and the worst dreams that ever I have are when I hear the surf booming about its coasts, or start upright in bed, with the sharp voice of Captain Flint still ringing in my ears: 'Pieces of Eight? Pieces of Eight?'

Was there always going to be dread, even after a happy ending?

◆

One thing that never failed to amaze me about growing up in Belfast was that, once I moved outside it, no one had ever heard of my family. We were, how shall I say, *unattached*. We did not belong anywhere else in Ireland, even though parts of the family could trace strong and direct links with County Fermanagh. Yet, once out of Belfast, we were effectively in no-man's-land – whatever about further afield in London or, histrionically, in Huguenot France. I found this significant because the few writers I started to know something about – Irish writers, I mean – seemed to have connections all over the place. Not only did they know each other, but they seemed to know every town and village throughout the country like the backs of their hands. And someone always knew them, too.

In contrast we – my family – were, outside the city walls, anonymous. This was not a self-conscious policy, but it was an accepted, almost desired state of affairs. Consequently, I suppose, I have always found the notion of an extended literary community somewhat troubling. While I can see the obvious benefits, the drawbacks are also powerfully there in the consoling rhetoric and fiction of an artistic genealogical vindication – 'tradition'.

So, more by accident than design, I met few writers in the late 1960s and early 1970s before moving to the west coast of Ireland. *That* randomness strikes me now as important. In Ireland, we are too willing to seek refuge in forced and artificial patrimonies of the soul. Some writers see their place in the sun through assuming a kind of respectful nativist pedigree out of which their literary 'selves' are spun.

Diffidence, as much as difference, threatens such piety. Whereas place of birth, for example, should mean nothing more or less than exactly *that*, it more often than not opens up a Chinese boxful of *clichés* conforming to expectations of what that part of the country, its people and literature are supposed to be like. Expectations, as we all know, can be great. They can also, however, turn into mean, self-perpetuating categories – what Samuel Beckett called 'book-keeping'. No wonder, in the face of such proverbially congested space, many writers this century either left Ireland or fought a bitter rearguard action against it.

If, like Beckett, they left, it was to find a style of life more in keeping with their own needs. If they stayed, like Patrick Kavanagh, they learned, or did not, how to cope, which often meant creating a *persona*, a mask.

Yet people, including writers, get on with their own lives as best they can and, of course, getting on with one's writing means paying little heed to boundaries on the map, *any* map. So for me, without straining credulity too far, Robert Lowell summered in Donaghadee, Wallace Stevens lived up the Cave Hill Road; Elizabeth Bishop sat downstairs on the 64 bus, and Constantine Cavafy could be seen, on a very clear day, walking down the Duncairn Gardens, minding his own business.

Meanwhile, outside the library steps, or in front parlours, people confessed to writing poems. In school once, the headmaster commented on the fact that someone in assembly had a poem published and his name 'If I am not mistaken . . .', which I hotly denied. Why the shame of self-effacement? Why not? Who should care about the person that writes but that person? It is the work that counts and what happens to it.

Then I moved to the west of Ireland and non-stop reading as the names dropped like a mighty roll call: Yeats . . . Joyce . . . Synge. Breakneck stuff about The Tower and Yeats working away there. Or Joyce in Market Street, skipping along.

Writing was what they did and were. Why all this other fuss? No wonder the novelist in north Belfast stood in the bus queue, briefcase and dapper overcoat, being just himself. Mr Kafka or Mr Faulkner. And then all the other writers that started to matter, like Robert Lowell, or the Italian poet Eugenio Montale, who wrote:

> Since my birth I have felt a total disharmony with the reality that surrounded me, the material of my inspiration could only be that disharmony.
> . . . What I do say is that any expression at all which has had a miraculous, liberating effect on someone – an effect of liberation and of understanding the world – has attained its goal and achieved form.

So it took the hundred miles and more between Belfast and Galway to get some balance right: for my work slowly to achieve form. Slowly the past, such as it was, is worked into perspective to find out about now, the great derided and abused present. Our talk is otherwise lost to the future and to some imaginary state not adequately imagined today in Ireland and, for such a small country, monstrously out of proportion, like Frankenstein's monster. All the protected resentment over the years; the little inhumanities; the cycles of hate: it was bound to break out at last in the 'Troubles' again. My own people, whoever they were, disappeared. Their work forgotten. Who hears from them now? And that must be the way of it. So when the writers move in, look out.

There is a moral there. We pick up the hoofbeats, the Iron Horse of History coming down the line. Time for change. Time for a change from everyone else's history to our own, which equals mine. This is the objective story whoever tells it. What does *me* matter but the telling?

◆

This is probably why the first part of my book of poems, *Sunday School* (1991) is set in north Belfast. But it is not so much the place that matters to me as the mood of a particular time there: the mid-1950s and early 1960s. The weight of that world has fascinated me – post-war, protestant – and the dominant view of the Cave Hill, always there, like the past itself, high above us. Whereas the lough lay seductively, promising adventure, and the hills beyond shone with sun and rain. *Sunday School* is, in part, about this world – its sense of scorn and disapproval; its inwardness and strength; its uncertainty and self-awareness; its cunning survival; its desperation.

In several of my poems, I have introduced the way in which the Bible formed, whether we liked it or not, a kind of natural moral backdrop to our young lives. Life was proverbial. We were told things through certain parables and I have found that this keeps cropping up in the poems I write. Some of the poems in my previous book, *The Lundys Letter* (1985), were similarly indebted to teachings from the Old Testament and, naturally, the images which remained with me of that time in church-going and school. 'The Bright Hour,' a sequence of poems from *Sunday School*, is like an album of the past and a young man's place within it. The title means, literally, a time put aside during the working day for religious contemplation and study. This sequence of poems, in my own mind at least, completes the first part of *Sunday School*.

I have always been intrigued by power, who holds it, what they do with it – its trappings, the way people express themselves. The vulgarity and emptiness of most wealthy people is what 'Speedboats 1972' is about; but also, too, the poem concerns the naïveté of our student days when we actually thought we could take on the world with posters:

> . . . on the sand-swept promenade below
> the burghers and their wives
> undress and hit the speedboats,
> carving up the bay between them.

As mentioned, I left Belfast in 1974 but, in a way, I only found out where it was after that. In poems like 'Local People', 'The Likelihood of Snow/The Danger of Fire', and 'Innocence', I tried to write out of this process of discovery as it happened. Whereas 'To My Inhaler', a quirky poem that has the line which gives *Sunday School* its title, turns the collection in a new direction – away from the cultural inheritance I was given towards a freer sense of the present, and the kind of writing, music and art to which I am drawn:

> One breathless night remembering it all
> from storybook pictures in Sunday School . . .
>
> . . . I played upon this alto of metered air
> and slowly the sounds cleared
> to our baby girl piping up
> in her own dark world.

Poets rarely are sure what they do. I, for one, never really know why I write the stuff I do. Poetry for me is a way of getting things clear; of sorting things out. I like the statement of Jacques Villon, the French painter, when he said: 'I seek to avoid confusion'. That is a good slogan to my way of thinking. Often, too, our own 'dark worlds' brighten through art. Marc Chagall, another painter whom I admire, has a famous painting of two lovers soaring above their village. He turns life upside down. Everything becomes fluid and possible. A few years ago, I was thinking of this and the exceptional weather we were having, for it never stopped raining. Three poems from the latter portion of *Sunday School*, which I see as a set – 'The Water Table', 'A Story' and 'One Summer' – move into a new world. But of all the poems in *Sunday School*, I am most proud of 'Safe Houses'. The poem shifts into the political climate and the terrible lassitude we are often forced to live in today.

Sunday School ends with several related poems which come from my current life living in Dublin. So much of that city reminds me of the Belfast suburbs I grew up in that I really find myself quite at home. So, too, with 'Straws in the

Wind' and 'The Just' my feelings for what 'home' can mean and where it is, come together. And a kind of obsession I have with the secrecy and privacy of people's lives – how that can be a great strength but also a danger too:

> I think I hear night-things bombard
> our fragile peace: straws in the wind,
> a fugitive dog sniffing the backsteps.

Many of the poems I have written try to answer this obsession. As Jacques Villon said, 'When one seeks, one cannot put precisely into words what he has not yet found.' The poems I write are about that search and about trying to find some kind of precision.

IV

I am not sure now whether we started the Lyric Youth Theatre in Belfast or just took it over for a while. By 'we' I mean a group of students at Orangefield Boys School in Belfast in the mid-1960s. We were taught by a marvellous man called Sam McCready. He it was who directed the fifth and sixth years in a dramatised version of Milton's *Paradise Lost*, featuring, amongst others, Brian Keenan, author of the international best-selling memoir, *An Evil Cradling* (1992).

There had been a tradition of staging plays at Orangefield, including a marvellous production of Molière's *Tartuffe*, directed by Mr Horner (I still can't bring myself to call him anything else). Also the street-songs and urban ballads of Belfast were preserved in class by David Hammond. And there were dances ('hops') on Saturday nights.

Of the arty generation at Orangefield, though, Sam McCready was the main man. We were into blues, R & B, anything we could get our hands on to read (Keats figured a lot for some reason), as well as dancing and partying. It was a great time. We were sulky know-it-alls, whose hero was Albert Camus, and we loved hanging loose outside the City Hall or the Wimpy Bar or the Steps of either the Linen Hall Library or the Central Library. We listened to Van Morrison on the transistor radio and thought we saw him getting the Gilnahirk bus. We went for what seemed like every day and night to Sammy Huston's Jazz Club, or the Maritime, or Betty Staffs, or the Plaza in the afternoons and thought the world would never end. The bands played on and on and on.

In 1966 it looked that way, at least. In only four years, of course, it was blown apart. But it was Sam McCready who during this time inspired some of us to write. I started to actually *show* my poems to people under his steady encouragement. We also went to dance classes given by Helen Lewis and eventually staged our first production at The Lyric Youth Theatre. It was Brecht's *Caucasian Chalk Circle*.

It was a great success. We played in The Opera House and many from that original company went ahead with theatre in one way or another. John Hewitt is acting in Belfast, Peter Quigley is directing and acting; every second advertisement you hear is probably voiced-over by Brian Munn; Gary Williamson went into set-design; Colin Lewis is at the BBC and a host of others kept faith with the ethos Sam developed by writing and acting.

I remember distinctly the little hall we gathered in on Cromwell Street, off Botanic Avenue, and the mystery as Brecht's play unfolded before our very eyes in the winter of 1967. We then took to the road.

In Pomeroy, Co Tyrone, bouncing around in the back of the Ulster Orchestra's truck, it really felt as if this was the true bohemian life. Arriving then into this strange village and building the set, before we were taken to a house and plied with tea and sandwiches. 'Are you whittlin'?' For a Belfast lad I could have been in a foreign country. Geoffrey Quigley adjudicated and in the refreshment room later, before we broke the set down, I remember looking around and seeing all my friends who were now actors and stage-hands and thinking this was for me. I applied to Guidhall but was too young and told I'd get in the next year. I went to London for a while and then returned to Belfast and hung around, but the group had broken up, more or less. My good friend, Gary had gone to Nottingham to study art. I finished my 'A' Levels and eventually went to college. I wrote more poems and started to publish and broadcast them.

For a young guy, in his mid-teens, the Youth Theatre at the Lyric was a new world opening out. While my grandmother taught poetry as elocution and singing as 'a good thing to do', the Youth Theatre became a way of life. Walking into the Lyric, going onto the stage, getting in behind the wings of the Opera House; sorting out the set in Pomeroy was for this kid of fifteen the real business. Twenty-five years later the love of theatre is still there, undiminished, though I guess I'm a little wiser about the vagaries of living as a writer.

◆

The only connection I had with any Belfast Group was with whoever went on stage at The Maritime, Sammy Houston's, Betty Staffs or any of the other clubs and dancehalls where Belfast groups played. The first time I heard of such as *The Belfast Group* I was well gone from the city and living in the west coast of Ireland. This is not to say that the individual names of *The Group* were unfamiliar. In about 1967 the head prefect at Orangefield gave a special class on Seamus Heaney's *Death of a Naturalist* and we all sat around being very cool when he quoted:

Right down the dam gross-bellied frogs were cocked
On sods; their loose necks pulsed like sails. Some hopped:
The slap and plop were obscene threats. Some sat
Poised like mud grenades, their blunt heads farting.

Whatever poetry was read during the 1960s in the Belfast I knew it wasn't Irish. I bought, in 1967, *W H Auden: The Penguin Poets*, selected by the author, and our school text was the mind-bending *Faber Book of Modern Verse*, edited by Michael Roberts (1965). I can also see from the library which has survived *Poetry of the Thirties*, introduced and edited by Robin Skelton, bought in November 1968; *The Mid Century: English Poetry 1940-60*, introduced and edited by David

Wright (1968) and George Steiner's *Penguin Book of Modern Verse Translation*, alongside *The New Poetry*, selected and introduced by A Alvarez and selling in 1967 for 4/6d.

The Beats, Russian poets like Akhmatova, all the Penguin Modern Poets series and Sylvia Plath made up the magic. Outside of Yeats, very very little was homegrown.

Poetry had, after all, to find a place alongside music, dancing and partying. The notion that there was *A Group* knocking around in the heart of Belfast discussing poetry (*'workshopping'* as it would now be called) seemed unbearably keen and much too open. If you wrote, best to keep it secret or wait until the late night blackout in the front room when the pals were laid back and you could speak out of the darkness about the future.

After a spell in London, and the return to Belfast, the Central Library steps, the Linen Hall Library, the Crown Bar, the Fiddler's, Olde House, Hercules, Spanish Rooms and Kelly's Cellars, a few names did circulate: Heaney, Longley and Mahon. But as to their constituting *A Group*, never mind *The Group*, it did not penetrate deepest north Belfast. Mention of The Group there meant a Theatre.

There may have been some sense that a group of poets from the north were publishing in London, and could be seen from time to time around the place; but this would have been after the event. Not being part of the literary scene, being turned on by music in those days – the late 60s – obviously meant our minds were elsewhere. Whatever we read was more likely to come from America and England than from Ireland and it had to compete with *NME* and *Melody Maker*.

When 'Ireland' came into view, it was traditional music, not the poetry of any Group. Indeed, at NUU, John Montague and Thomas Kinsella had a much deeper presence than *'The Group'*. This was, after all, the first college in the north where Student Union Minutes were recorded in English *and* Irish.

The political warning systems were on full alert from 1972, the year that Derek Mahon's *Lives* appeared and in that slimmest of volumes the non-Groupie seemed to get it absolutely right:

> Spring lights the country: from a thous-
> and dusty corners, house to house,
> from under beds and vacuum cleaners,
> empty Kosangas containers,
> bread bins, car seats, crates of stout,
> the first flies cry to be let out;
> to cruise a kitchen, find a door
> and die clean in the open air.

The Group were consigned to myth and thesis-mongers, despite protests from those who had little to do with it. I suppose the idea that an artistic cell can reside within the body politic is fatally alluring to the literary historian. Upon this seedbed other names were added and before you know it a self-sustaining extended family comes into critical being called *Northern Poets*. Without *The Group*, the notion of Northern Poetry cannot exist, except as a moment of historical coincidence and not cultural identity.

The books of poems tell another story altogether: the imaginative gulf that separates Longley from Heaney, for instance. There is the temporary loss to view of Stewart Parker and the deplorable amnesia surrounding the role that Padraic Fiacc played in his Glengormley home encouraging many local and visiting poets and prose-writers during the early 1960s. And before him John Hewitt, Roy McFadden, Sam Hanna Bell and so on.

We lack the history, so what has taken its place is the consolation of anecdote, and the curiosity of foreign researchers.

If Belfast needed *The Group*, did the poets need Belfast? Who can say? Whatever The Group meant, only Michael Longley remained to carry the very real burdens of the city through the treacherous 1970s and '80s.

Some day, too, an enterprising young writer will explore what was happening in Belfast throughout the present century, as writer, artist, musician, dancer, singer, chinked this way and that to find an authentic voice. Derek Mahon's 'Glengormley' might be a good place to start:

> I should rather praise
> A worldly time under this worldly sky —
> The terrier-taming, garden-watering days
> Those heroes pictured as they struggled through
> The quick noose of their finite being. By
> Necessity, if not choice, I live here too.

What 'here' meant to those writers associated with *The Group* is the persistently *unasked* question because Belfast has historically been seen as the kiss of death to artistic ambition. In reaction to the other capital city, Dublin, it looks, on the face of it, that Belfast was waiting its turn to play host to a generation of writers. That the greatness associated with Dublin's literary past was almost totally due to those writers who fled the city (Wilde, Shaw, Joyce, Synge, Beckett) should not blind us to the crucial difference in Belfast's culture which Derek Mahon commented upon in an article called 'Poetry in Northern Ireland', published in *20th Century Studies* (November 1970):

> There are many ways in which poets can be contrasted and compared, but in the Northern Irish situation . . . there is an obvious line to be drawn . . . the difference of religious background, as always in Ireland, is not so much important in itself as it is an indication of political, therefore national, therefore cultural allegiance, or lack out of it.

Irish writing was almost immobilised by these critical terms of *allegiance* to place. Rather than examining the nature of allegiance in a writer's life, or indeed the places themselves, far too much was read into the random and arbitrary happening of a phenomenon such as *The Group* when a few people who wrote poetry gathered to talk about what they were doing, before going back out again into the world.

V

All my people are protestant with their roots in the Huguenots from France who fled persecution in the eighteenth century and settled in Ireland somewhat later. My middle name – which used to drive me daft when the schoolmaster read it out from the attendance register – is Chartres. There is another refugee, Quartz, who married Chartres along with Bradshaws and Darraghs in the family lists.

I went to Sunday School and Church, joined the Scouts and lived a fairly typical boy's life growing up in the civil society of north Belfast: playing football, marking every season's changes with a different game, walking the streets, talking and smoking. I had no complaints. The world I knew was the world that I took for granted: 'This was the way it was' as Van Morrison says. Our district was predominantly protestant: we had very good neighbours, some catholic, some Jewish and other refugees who had married soldiers stationed in Europe during the war. There was a synagogue, two grand Church of Ireland churches, Baptist halls, Kingdom Hall, one catholic Church and so on.

My great-grandfather lived most of his life on the Duncairn Gardens. He was dead before I arrived on the scene but his influence was very strong through his daughter, Ethel, my grandmother with whom I lived. His name was Billy Chartres and he worked for *The Belfast Telegraph* and *Ireland Saturday Night*. He was a staunch Unionist who had signed the 1912 Covenant, was a city-father and leading member of the Orange Order of his day and was an obsessive football man, having helped set up the Junior League. As a journalist he wrote under the name *The Wanderer* – which might have something to do deep down with his own family's spiritual roots as refugees at one time, or it may not.

Anyway, it took a long time to sort out what this invisible man meant to me. Although, as I say, I never met him, he lived in my mind and through photographs, press cuttings, cartoons and some family reminiscences, it took me ages to realise that William Bailey Chartres – to give him his full name – represented the past to me. He it was who dramatised the history of my immediate surroundings; he was the tradition that I could have followed having thought about going for a job as a 'cub' reporter at *The Telegraph* in the late 1960s. When I left Belfast in 1974 he travelled with me, like a shade, and I have had endless imaginary encounters with this Billy Chartres ever since, rebuking and chastising me, and ending up like Alfred Hitchcock walking through my poems when he gets half a chance!

Often critics and journalists talk about northern protestants as if they were dour, narrow, bigoted, unimaginative, mean, spiteful and so on. I am sure many are: as many as there are in any community in any place in the world. I get seriously fed up with the way journalists – with some honourable exceptions – and writers these days either pillory or patronise ordinary protestants from Belfast as *culture-less*. I think of William Bailey Chartres and the family he came from and the one that came from him, which includes me, or the friends and their families whom I knew growing up in this city. Whatever about their faults, or our faults, I do not see them the way they are portrayed so generally by the media. While it might involve a bit of hard work, like basic historical research, it doesn't take long to show the intellectual, cultural, musical, philosophical and artistic traditions that lie buried beneath the imprisoning stereotypical images with which we are all too often treated in this part of the country.

Be that as it may, it took me a long time to understand that Billy Chartres was, in fact, my past and I had better try and understand it rather than run away from it. Which takes me to my third point: I am also a poet, or, if you prefer, I write poems. I don't do this for a living because I couldn't afford to, but I have been writing poems since I was about fourteen. It is one of the most important things in my life. I also write about poetry and the cultural and political world which poets inhabit. I would prefer just to do nothing else but that can become terribly introverted.

The first poems I wrote were about nothing much but a young man's infatuation with language. They were written in the attic bedroom where I lived, looking out over Brantwood,

Grove Park, Seaview, the Shore Road and the Lough. These landscapes slowly asserted themselves in my poems the further I went away from them.

I read everything I could and was particularly drawn to American poets like Robert Lowell. Eventually some of my poems were published in *The Irish Press* in Dublin (there didn't seem to be anywhere to publish them in Belfast then). Some were broadcast on BBC Radio Ulster, read by Denys Hawthorne and J.D. Devlin. Others were published in an anthology edited by Seamus Heaney called *Soundings* and published by Belfast's Blackstaff Press. By the mid-1970s I was publishing poems in Britain and further afield and in 1978 my first book of poems, *Sheltering Places* was published by Blackstaff.

Now the point I want to make is that it was only *after* this time, after this late apprenticeship if you like, that I started to actually think about what I was doing: of seeing the connection between Belfast, protestantism and poetry. The Billy Chartres phenomenon. It hit me like an electric shock. It took seven years, from 1978 to 1985, living in Galway, starting a family, trying to find work, experiencing life there, travelling back and forth to Belfast, trying to explain what was going on – it took seven years before Billy Chartres and I came to terms with each other.

My poems cannot be anything other than what they are. The Old Testament, the legacy of British military history, customs; the attitudes and experiences and desires of all the people I grew up with in the early 1950s and '60s are at the very core of what I write. Maybe the poems I am writing now are freer as a result, but that is another day's work.

My belief is that poets are poets first and citizens second. No matter what the religion, genre or race, poetry is the thing that matters. When people, be they politicians or professional commentators, proclaim that poets *should* write about this or that, that the poet *must* identify with this community or that – you had better watch out. Because we are no longer talking about art but propaganda. Poetry, like music, or dance, or painting, or football for that matter, thrives when it is given its own space and hasn't some well-meaning, or not so well-meaning, guru breathing down your neck. My poems are addressed to whosoever has the chance and cares to listen.

I think of my poems in the same terms as Herman Melville comments in *Moby-Dick*, or *The Whale*: 'All these things are not without their meaning'. I hate stereotypes. I hate the way Belfast is treated. I hate the one-upmanship and jockeying for position between different groups as if 'culture' could ever belong to one side to the disadvantage of the other. The basic truth about culture and art is that it cannot be segregated or worn like a badge of identity. It becomes something else then, like a slogan. I hate all the tired, stale old arguments about this sense of identity being more natural, or historically valid than another – as if there was some Superman-like Kryptonite which we have to possess to make us great or, at least, greater than the next. Writing poems, finding the language to do it best in, the forms and the voice, is difficult enough.

VI

In the springtime of 1973 the Belfast writer Brendan Hamill introduced me to Padraic Fiacc. Brendan was, like myself, a student at the fledgling University of Ulster, but he knew just about everyone who was writing in or about the north. Fiacc, he said, was thinking of doing an anthology on the north. I was writing and publishing poems here and there and so, we should meet.

I hadn't actually met many poets up to that time. In fact, I don't think I knew any, so this meeting with Fiacc was very important. He lived in the end house in a row of typical suburban houses on the outskirts of Belfast. His home had been a stop-over, at one time or another, for many of Ireland's best-known writers. Fiacc himself had been close to Padraic Colum. He was a very real link between the lost world of the Revival and the disintegrating world of Belfast. He also knew the work of Joyce (Fiacc's first book was called *By the Black Stream*, after Joyce's poem 'Tilly'), Beckett, most of the Classics, European writers like Mauriac, Baudelaire and there was that poem of Derek Mahon's, 'Glengormley' (the suburb where he lived) dedicated to Fiacc and published in Mahon's first collection, *Night-Crossing* (1968).

After our first meeting, I made a point whenever I was in town of seeing Joe (for he reverted to his real name when the defences went down and he became Joe O'Connor again). We would sit in the living room and talk about 'the situation' ie. The Troubles, which was turning from bad to the worst it could be; and the domestic chores which he religiously went through (lighting fires, clearing the garden of leaves, making coffee, spotting the return of birds, putting the 'garbage' out) concealed an obsessed artistic temperament that was struggling with the break-up of both his personal and social life.

What was going on in Belfast in 1973-74 makes for grim reading with nightly assassinations, bombings and a net of fear cast over the city. When I finished my studies at NUU, driving from Belfast to Coleraine through the UDA barricades of the Ulster Workers' strike, I took the job in the Fine Arts Department at Belfast's Central Library. Every week, one or more of us would visit Joe; sometimes there would be gatherings. At one of these I met a young lad called Gerry McLoughlin, who wrote under the name of Gerry Locke.

He was like the rest of us. A Belfast lad who loved literature but couldn't sort out how it could relate to what was going on around him. When Joe's anthology, *The Wearing of the Black*, was published by The Blackstaff Press, I had left Belfast and was living in Galway, studying at UCG. My girl and I travelled up on 14th December 1974 by train, Galway to Dublin, Dublin to Belfast. The party the next day was the last time we were to see Gerry McLoughlin. He was murdered four months later on the 7th April, 1975. His murder changed everything and it represents a terrible watershed in all our lives. I turned my back for several years on Belfast and the sickening reality of sectarianism.

Joe visited us in Galway. He was devastated but slowly his writing lead him to a way out, or is it in?

There is no other poet like Padraic Fiacc who knows the cost of Irish history and has suffered as a result. All the faddish talk about inner exile, violence, post-colonialism and so forth; all the business about the supremacy of our own colloquial voices; the image of the marginalised writer: all these issues we hear and read so much about find in Padraic Fiacc's poetry their first substantive expression.

A few years ago, an old friend of mine (and Joe's), Aodán MacPóilin, suggested we should make a selection: *Ruined Pages: Selected Poems of Padraic Fiacc* is the result. As a bonus we also included a marvellous programme Joe wrote in 1980 for Paul Muldoon at BBC Northern Ireland called 'Hell's Kitchen'.

Padraic Fiacc's poetry is the lasting testament to the human spirit that kept Belfast from turning into Sarajevo. On a very personal level, he bridged for me, as a young poet in the early 70s, the link between poetry and violence – a link that underpinned my own first book of poems. It's difficult after twenty-five years to recall the mood and even the time when I wrote most of the poems that were gathered into *Sheltering Places*. I had taken with me to Galway a notebook full of things I was then working on in 1974, along with poems which had appeared when I was a student at the New University.

I had two little pamphlets of poems published in 1976. One was called *Heritages*, published in the Isle of Skye by a company called Aquila, and the other was a sequence of poems called after Yeats (who else!) *Blood and Moon* and it came out with the original Lagan Press. You never see either of these pamphlets nowadays but it was from amalgamating them, and adding on some new poems that I had written in Galway, that a manuscript went up to Blackstaff Press and when they decided to publish, I was delighted.

We travelled up by train and stayed at Orangefield before heading across to the Upper Newtonards Road and into what was Jim and Diana Gracey's house. Anne Tannahill had just joined the Blackstaff team and, having signed the contract, my first, we left, all in a bit of a daze, stepping over Montezuma, the big ginger cat, and out home.

Sheltering Places was published in May 1978 and I gave a reading (my second) in Galway above a bicycle shop during the (second) Galway Arts Festival. We had book covers but nothing inside and I quaked all the way through the reading. In a couple of years the book went out of print and stayed that way until 1993 when it was reissued to coincide with a remarkable exhibition of images by Noel Connor drawn from *Sheltering Places* and also a sequence of my poems from the 1980s called *Company*.

Noel had written to me when he was preparing a book for Bloodaxe called *Confounded Language*, and mentioned how the poems in *Sheltering Places* had stayed with him, reminding him of the Belfast of the early 1970s. Belfast looked like Berlin during the war; street-lights smashed, the town at night a deserted wasteland; no buses; the bars and cinemas shut early. And people had more or less withdrawn into their own districts, not to move out when darkness fell.

Noel wrote in one of his letters:

> Immersing myself in the poems again revived all my initial reactions – dislocation and desolation; a sense of being stranded in the wrong place with no return journey possible; anger and admiration. The images are a response to the mood of the whole collection.

I had been tinkering with the poems myself when Noel wrote and asked could he do something with them. I sent him the revised version and just waited to see what would come of it.

The images which Noel created capture the ominous, lurking, fearful mood that many of the poems were written in and against. The 'chair' which is the most basic of Noel's images changes from being an ordinary domestic functional thing, into alternative presences. It is a retreat; it is a ghastly thing, on fire, it is a pathetic, lost thing; it is something returning to nature; it is shadowed by perverse contrasts, such as the castle steps; it breaks up and almost disappears.

In these ways Noel had, I see now, delved into the core experience of that time in the early 1970s. For many the time was manic, totally unpredictable, crazy, with bombs exploding all over the place and streets collapsing into the streets. And it didn't really seem feasible to write poems. The pressure was internalised so if that was what you wanted to do (write poems), somehow or other you had to learn how to make sense of the civic chaos you were living.

Reading the poems now, they strike me as being very harsh with themselves and, at the same time, innocent and shocked. I don't think anyone really discussed these things then. In fact I don't think we *discussed* anything really; not the way of today, that is for sure.

I suppose, given the state of Belfast, people were living at a weird and distorting angle to 'normality' which had itself become normal, or at least, more common. Indeed the post-modern boredom that set in throughout the 1980s (when politics was emptied of meaning by Thatcher and Reagan) would have been inconceivable in the early to mid-70s. *That* earnestness looks old-fashioned now, and is generally misread as such by those whose patience with the northern Irish business has worn thin.

The poems in *Sheltering Places* were written without a clue why. They were not shown to anyone and they had nothing to do with being part of any 'group' or 'school'. I think the same goes for Noel Connor and his artwork.

When he left nationalist Andersonstown for art college in England, it was the same trip which I took when I left loyalist Ballybeen for university in Coleraine. Noel tells the story himself of waving goodbye in the combat jacket and not having a notion what the next step was.

VII

I was sitting in a room in what has effectively become a forgotten part of the west of Ireland, a town battered around between pillar and post – a town, to all intents and purposes, no longer sure what to make of itself.

Around me were in-laws, my wife and daughter. The talk was hectic, it being some time since we had visited my mother-in-law, her sister and her brother, all of whom were in their eighties. The gathering was in the small living room that looks out to a main road. The talk drifted unpredictably from one thing to another, with the past like a rudder, shifting us this way and that. Of Collins and who had killed him; of England during the War, where my aunt had worked as a district nurse; of weaver-fish, whose reactive prongs can poison and numb an arm for months; of life in gaol during the War of Independence; of a returned distant relative and his family; of recent deaths and how they stripped the town of more of the old inhabitants, remnants, if you will, of this century in a part of Ireland – people who had experienced its history first-hand, participated in some of it but for the rest were outside and resigned, their feeling for history and politics determined by that place.

I was sitting in the room listening and, after a while, I turned the radio on and heard someone discuss 'Poetry and Modern Society'. The difference was immediate.

With the room so full of talk (details of history, fragments of politics, of de Valera's head looking like that of an Indian, of the weather and how it was changing – such amazing variety and intensity), the sheer cacophonous energy was of many voices telling their own story all seeking to be heard. And here on the radio was one voice, calm and controlled, being listened to, presumably with interest, in various homes, flats and rooms throughout the country.

The contrast is stark and severe but it does portray the kind of forces with which a poet must deal. Maybe not at the level of an individual poem, a specific image or scene, but in the backroom of the imagination, where poems are first made and developed; that clambering-for-expression, with its own vitality and insistence, exerts a special influence on what a poet writes.

This influence leads in 'two directions' at the same time – away from the gaggle of Babel's tower but also towards it, trying to hold those elements of it with which one can cope. Rarely is there a 'satisfactory' balance. The poet is confined to only a part of speech.

A poet today, and possibly always, tries to make a poem that is entire and complete, unlike life where failure, defeat, injustice and pain so often interrupt and snatch our freedom away. This is not to suggest that poets and poetry in the modern world must necessarily speak as if success, triumph, equality, hope and love were abandoned concepts. Far from it.

I don't want to sound like an evangelist. Hope, love, injustice are just words, abstractions in the same way that the word 'language' is when related to the scene I opened with. I think too of another scene.

It is 1960 or thereabouts in the sitting room of a red-bricked house in a terraced row of seven houses, wedged between Belfast's Cave Hill and the Lough: a world of small gardens, minute backyards; our dilapidated scullery and two flights of creaking stairs that lead past the bathroom, like a look-out post. The mock stained-glass spangling light on the landing with two bedrooms, their fireplaces blocked, huge wardrobes and uncertain windows and my own den at the top of the house, with its slanting ceilings, the piles of family mementoes and sheet music stashed in the corner and the chimney always alive with sparrows.

In the front room, a large mirror leans above the mantelpiece before which a baize card-table is placed. To its right, a closed Steinway piano, and to the left a bay-window basking in the last of the late afternoon light. You can hear, just about, the tock of a grandfather clock on the landing. Also my grandmother's voice instructing a young girl from the district how to recite a poem properly. It is Wednesday: elocution class.

Ethel, light-opera singer, shop-assistant, belle, has in front of her Palgrave's *Treasury* opened at 'The Daffodils'. The girl, one of many, speaks the words with urgent feeling, the stresses and inflections in keeping with convention. The girl watches her own mouth in the mirror as Ethel mouths the syllables in a prompting mime.

For Ethel, it is a love and a profession. She taps out the rhythm like a conductor. The poem sings in a controlled and articulate manner. It has been mastered and the girl, in a pretty dress, will win a little cup and go into the world confident of the way she speaks, vowels like balloons, the head swaying ever so slightly from side to side. Until, probably, marriage, and the certain slow reclaiming of her own accent from that sophisticated gloss which did not really help her 'get on' in the world after all.

This scene, an amalgam of many I witnessed as a small boy in my grandmother's house, opening doors to the hopeful and ambitious, comes to my mind when I think of the rigorous way poets must understand the discipline of their craft. And here too, both scenes play across each other – the helter-skelter of impressions; the mannered poise; the fragments and figments of history; the cultivated grace; the nationalist west; the unionist north-east – each entailing its own hurt and insecurities, pride and prejudice, and how these are expressed differently.

This is where the poet comes in, uncalled-for, but there all the same, summarising the complexity as best as he or she can, discerning what is humanly possible. The poet deals, in other words, with freedom. And in a world such as our own, which has many freedoms claimed on its behalf but few realised, poets are bound to come up against the stone wall of this contradiction. The poets' response tells a lot, too, about the environment they find themselves in – do they recoil embittered from it into a dismissive posture, shunning the outside world? What place have they in the ordinary scheme of things? Do they reject that place in pursuit of a different lifestyle more in keeping with ideas about poetry's so-called 'marginalised' role in society – the imagination hounded out of existence, fighting a last ditch battle against materialism or some such foe? These questions have addled the finest of poetic sensibilities, but is this not shunting us into the sterile debate about 'what is relevant today?' Nothing is ever relevant for a writer until the writer makes it so. Before that can happen, it must be 'relevant' to his or her self, and just because something is deemed relevant does not necessarily mean it will be artistically valuable.

The greatest influence on a writer is the past. Its relevance is pervasive and often it is only when that past is unearthed beneath the rubble of today, that a poet begins to make sense of his or her own imaginings. Somehow the recovery of the world of the past not only helps a poet show what makes up the world but also helps make it a more 'liveable' place in the here and now. In this sense, a poet is strictly 'anti-nostalgic'.

In my own case, most of my poems are about this process, whether they are set in a boarding house in County Down, a burnt-out street in Belfast, Maam Cross, the front garden, an imaginary church, or in no particular place at all. It is the voices of mood and the objective turn of events which fascinate me, how they live in our memory, unsettling, probing, making us think and feel in certain ways. And if memory is, as William Carlos Williams called it in his poem 'The Descent', 'a kind of accomplishment/a sort of renewal/even/an initiation', so much the better. Poetry becomes a necessary ritual, not so much a possession or a note of 'High Art'; not a filler-in for festivals or the exclusive hallmark of a dedicated individual or band of individuals cultivated by and for an uninterested society. Poetry makes common cause with the ordinary in quite unexpected and exceptional ways. This is not lip-service to that old sloppy notion of 'The Poet as Public Spokesperson'. Such self-appointments invariably end up in lifeless rhetoric, soft-centred lyricism and preordained ways of seeing and saying things.

It is a question of balance, instinct and example. This transcends every kind of border, is dynamic and political. I think of Carlos Williams' great poem 'Asphodel, That Greeny Flower' – direct and poetic, it brings out the difficult truth of writing poetry, the knowledge and beauty it can discover and the strange relentless power it has to show us what we are or think we are:

Of Asphodel, that greeny flower,
     I come, my sweet,
         to sing to you!

My heart rouses
     thinking to bring you news
         of something

that concerns you
     and concerns many men. Look at
         what passes for the new.

You will not find it there but in
     despised poems.
         It is difficult

to get the news from poems
     yet men die miserably every day
         for lack

of what is found there.
     Hear me out
         for I too am concerned

and every man
     who wants to die at peace in his bed
         besides.

PART FOUR

◆

A CHILD OF THE EMPIRE

I

When I was growing up in north Belfast in the 1950s London was our second home. Half our family had emigrated to the English capital early on in the century and there was a regular tooing and frooing from London where my great aunt and her extended family lived. We travelled by boat and train and eventually by air. We attended weddings and funerals, holidayed there, and I lived there for a while before opting for Belfast in the late 1960s.

As Belfast protestants, not of the churchy or party-political type, Britain existed as England. It was the cyclorama to our lives. We listened to BBC on the radio, and watched BBC and ITV when the time came. Our house retained the black-out blinds from World War II up to the late 1950s. The bottled sauces and Indian tea, Camp coffee and medicines, brandnamed jumpers and socks, Tate and Lyle Golden Syrup with its sleeping lion and sleepier slogan, Christmas cake and boxes of biscuits were all British made. My toys, too, and comics and footballs.

When it came to school, our history was British and the songs (along with accompanying gestures) which we were taught by the slightly electric Miss Gray were English and Scottish ballads:

> My body lies over the ocean
> My body lies over the sea
> My body lies over the ocean
> O bring back my body to me

The fact that it was *bonnie* seems to have passed us by. And the headmaster of my primary school, the mythopoetically named Mr Nelson, reputed to have looked exactly the same when my uncle attended, a generation earlier, walked about with a raffish stoop and had, in his small unlit office, two memorable symbols – a fighter-plane on a perspex mantle and a globe of the world demarcating the Empire. He was a proud, dignified and tolerant man so far as we could tell, and he never seemed to interfere in our lives. On the other hand, the teacher who looked like Clark Gable, spoke with a distinct twang under the voluptuous moustache, and smoked Senior Service, bore all the marks of a devil-me-care veteran. The War was the centrepiece in our upbringing. Its effects on the Belfast of my boyhood were clear. Behind our house, the Brickies – a derelict site; above us, the deserted US Army installation – a warren of outhouses and garages; away below us, *Prefabs* which housed hundreds of families whose homes had been destroyed when Belfast was blitzed in 1941.

And the stories of my great grandmother sitting through the Blitz under the stairs, giving out to the Jerries as an unexploded bomb lodged in the back wall; my grandmother working in an ammunitions factory, ducking IRA bullets; my mother's romance with a touring Army bandsman, and the men you could see and hear throughout the fifties and sixties, on the buses late at night, or stumbling home of an evening, regimental blazers and grey flannels, talking away to themselves or to their indignant yet knowing wives. These images have a life of their own and I will be keeping them in the back of my mind in what follows.

II

Cultural self-consciousness is fast becoming a civil service, literary duty and academic obligation. What was once an accent, an idiom, a voice turns into community action, a manifesto, a speech; a categorical imperative. There is nothing inherently 'wrong' in all this, so long as it is not predicated upon social engineering. For cultural identity has itself become a term much used and abused. In Ireland, it is thrown around like a frizbee. Terms such as Irish, British; nationalist, unionist; protestant, catholic. But what does identity actually mean, or, more importantly, are people really so preoccupied with it in Ireland as compared with people in England, France or the US? Certainly, with the firebreak of the ceasefires, the first real signs of political reality broke through 25 years of noxious and suffocating insularity. But like most people in Ireland I have been a spectator at the game, not even sure of the rules or the players.

Observing what is happening in and to one's country can be a strange and estranging sensation. It can be a bizarre experience listening to language being put through the mill. From my own experience, for instance, when a unionist politician talks about 'Eire' as a poor, backward country, run by priests, I have to pinch myself. Is this the same place where I have lived for the past 20 years? The loyalist notion that the Irish state is massing on the border, either physically, metaphysically, or constitutionally, to take over Ulster, that jewel in the crown, is simply mind-altering. Whereas republican rhetoric about an Ireland 'Gaelic and Free', a proud and sorrowful nation weeping and/or dancing at the crossroads, is in as sorry a state of delusion when compared with the reality and cultural priorities of the Republic, here-and-now. I suppose this compares with the dream-world which many in England still inhabit concerning the 'Great' in Great Britain, the 'United' in United Kingdom with the 'might' of mighty England at the very centre.

Whatever about the incontrovertible right of spokespersons to entertain such views, the fact that people have *killed* and *died* for versions thereof in Ireland and England is chillingly beyond belief. Like many others who consider themselves British, the protestants of Northern Ireland, who have kept themselves insulated in the comforting nostalgia called 'The British Empire', will need to step into the actual world. For a start they should recognise what has happened to and in Britian during the years of the 'Troubles'. When the Thatcherite era imploded, shattering along the way national institutions and civic assumptions and services, what was left was a demoralised, unemployable underclass, a confused educational system, a health system in crisis, a civic environment raped by privatisation, a political caste tarnished by financial corruption and enfeebled by the lack of any vision whatsoever and a culture weak in the public confidence to debate within itself its own future. More so than at any previous time this century, there is now a radical (visionary, if you like) challenge of re-imagining all the constituent parts of England, Scotland, Wales and their ties with Ireland. This does not mean abandoning the past and all those influences and experiences which hundreds of thousands, indeed millions, share at various different levels throughout the islands. Specifically, the cultural history of the northern protestants is a complex and challenging history, emblematic of much that is repressed in the Ireland of today and embarrassing in its militant nostalgia to the intellectual and media elite of England.

Sadly, all too often, their story, the protestant story, is patronised or distorted by journalists and other writers who are frustrated by the seemingly time-locked nature of the northern protestant culture, as if it only paralleled (or parodied) the intellectual complacency and inertia of the English establishment.

Protestants who believe in the union, who see, in other words, London as their capital, and Manchester, Birmingham, Leeds, Edinburgh, Glasgow as like-minded and 'British' as themselves, and all those who believe in democratic rights, should have absolutely nothing to lose, or fear, from speaking their mind on the arguments about why the union should *remain*. Far too often however all one hears from Belfast and London is rant about a mysterious cultural 'link' while outdated nationalist rhetoric obscures the acute, deep-seated economic and cultural realities which continue to bind both islands together, howsoever political history has driven them apart.

My own deepest wish, for what it is worth, is that along the way to peace and justice the genuine *common* traditions and experience of northerners is reclaimed from the nightmare of the past. It would be foolhardy to assume, however, that cultural reprogramming and therapy will do the trick; as if unionists who are protestant are merely closet Irish who need to come out. Many already see themselves as Irish. And many more do not. Others see themselves as British *and* Irish. So what? Is there not a community known as Irish-American? 'Hybridity', where are you now when we need you?

Undoubtedly after much pain, anger and uncertainty, protestants are coming to the realisation that they have to reconsider their past, not as a gesture of 'sell out' or 'compromise' but simply as an exercise in influencing what the future may hold: effectively an exercise in revision which lies before us all. Marooned within their own statelet for so long, ordinary protestants had no other imaginative stability than that bequeathed to them through the turbulent 1910s and 20s by the unexplored and hasty formulations of James Craig and Edward Carson.

Since the foundation of that northern state the stultifying patronage of a distant, ignorant and uninterested imperial centre (London) viewed the provincial northern capital (Belfast) with bemused distaste. The institutional bigotry and injustice of the state was allowed to stew over four decades. This was matched by the congenitally suspect nationalism of what was once called the Free State which simply could not embrace the differences within the putative nation and was even to make a virtue out of refusing to imagine the problems which were storing up in the north of Ireland.

In this sense, the protestants of the north saw themselves in splendid isolation, a perpetual adolescence peripheral to the critical focus of definition which did not involve them. They were heard, but not seen. They acted accordingly, and have always been seen as a belligerent and beleaguered third party, reacting to the various realignments which have taken place between the dominant two partners of 'Ireland' and 'England'. No matter what 'solution' is arrived at it seems that they will more than likely remain outside it; against the current. They are also symbols of a deeper malaise confounding both countries. By their very existence they threaten easy notions of cultural unity *inside* Ireland while reminding post-industrial England of its colonialist and imperial past. Indeed, it is not stretching credibility too far to suggest that the protestants summon up the problems which lie ahead for *England* if and when a written constitution and a radically revisioned state become a central and necessary part of the political agenda. The difficulties which the northern protestants are experiencing in the present, anticipates the internal wrangling and doubts the English will have to go through if they are to find new, enabling mythologies for a secular, multicultural republic embracing Scotland and Wales.

Saying the words 'a secular, multicultural republic' in the present climate of English debate makes the very idea seem far-fetched and urgent, at the same time. No wonder then that the protestant community, in rejecting a comparable possibility of an Irish republic, were caricatured as introverted, imaginatively dull and uncreative: terms by which the English are often similarly defined. Everywhere the northern protestant community turned, its self-image was distorted, like the mirrors in a carnival, into grotesque parody: loud-mouthed invective, *'anti'* everything, untranscendent, glum.

This short-circuit – which is a complicated and fascinating example of cultural amnesia and artistic-distortion – disempowered writers and artists within their own culture such as Louis MacNeice, Sam Hanna Bell, Sam Thompson and many others from the 1930s up to comparatively recent times.

It was a failure of educational will, critical blindness and institutional complacency on a massive scale going back generations, impacting upon the entire northern community. The effects however were particularly disabling for the protestant sense of culture, missing as it did, an immediate access to the counterweight of Irish literary and cultural traditions while averting its gaze from the US and, when the time came, Europe.

Out of such uncertainties and contradictions, the stereotypical clichés of 'Britishness' vis-à-vis 'Irishness' in the north were eventually fed back into the eruption of civil unrest. The buried prejudices which grew out of the absurdly partitioned Irish state came to haunt the country with a vengeance, and we have been paying for these bloody mistakes of the 1920s ever since and on all sides of the Irish Sea.

Some take arrogant satisfaction in this situation, the SHIP THE PRODS BACK mentality; others see northern protestant intransigence as one example of those historical facts and cultural conditions which need imaginative exploration, not exploitation. The shout of hundreds of thousands of northern protestants WE ARE BRITISH is loudest in an effort to convince themselves of the fact; it is a collective whistling in the dark – emotional, deep-seated, involuntary. The icons, flags and emblems of the British state are revered all the more intensely and intimately at such times when their self-belief and concepts of right are rubbished. There are parallels which can be pursued between the northern protestant situation today, and what might emerge in England in, say, 25 years when ordinary English men and women can no longer *take for granted* the stability and reliability of a given history and a cultural identity based unthinkingly upon the past. The English are living in an interregnum, but facing the wrong way around.

Depressingly, many of the clichés surrounding the northern protestant culture are recycled in England as much as in the Republic of Ireland, and further afield in the US. I could cite numerous examples, both personal and professional but one will suffice.

In 1994 *The Guardian* (16 July) ran a feature article called 'An Irish Answer' which was billed as 'a look beyond the prevailing images of northern culture'. The article merely reproduced the stale arguments about 'relating to' the Troubles before the author asserts:

> To find artistic fulfilment [means] to look beyond confines of the protestant world. To remain in a world where 'culture' is restricted to little more than flute-bands, Orange marches and the chanting of sectarian slogans at football matches.

The arrogance of all this ('little more') is staggering but not, alas, very surprising. Not one mention of the many writers, historians, scientists, musicians, medics, who have come from that 'protestant world'.

Imagine if these terms were used to describe the Irish or West Indian community in England, what justifiable rage there would be against such gross caricatures. Yet it is what writers have consistently had to face in Ireland (irrespective of the community from which they come) when stereotypes and cultural imperatives eclipse critical enquiry into actual artistic accomplishment and ambition. The significance of this *unease* plays across the cultural and political life of Belfast, London and Dublin and it will intensify confusingly when the stakes of revision (in terms of cultural authority and prestige) mount higher in the years ahead.

Indeed it is tempting to see *most* contemporary writing from Ireland as forever folkloric, underpinned by regional and/or national loyalties, political designs and social categorism. This, of course, is folly because it toys with the idea that politics can be conjured out of cultural roots at will. A fate the Irish have experienced in full measure may await the English as 'Englishness' literally becomes a thing of the past.

One is not a poet, but an Irish poet, (or a northern/protestant) and before you have opened your mouth, certain expectations and assumptions flick before the audience's mind. National myths, in other words, undergoing renovation and revision can turn into a spider's web, catching the individual artist's right to write with freedom out of his or her own self.

'The Aunt's Story', the opening poem of my collection, *Heart of Hearts* (1995) is about my being in London in 1963. I was both a stranger and a subject, conscious, like millions of others, of my difference, yet also feeling partly at home. It slowly dawned on me, as Neal Ascherson comments on a similar experience in his marvellous collection of essays, *Games With Shadows* (1988), that 'my sense of awe at the Providence which had mysteriously allotted me Britishness – that had gone'. 'The Aunt's Story' is about such a realisation, as loss and as liberation:

That first time in London, a family wedding.
I had my new school uniform on
and Great Uncle Bill stood in the perfect garden
of his home telling me to spell *character*.
The cats sat blinking in a far-off corner
and Eileen – *she never lost the accent* –
watched her sister's grandson perform.
The sky was bright as could be.

What walked in the shadow was The War,
the long road back, the swish of evening gowns,
as the girls crept in late to the god-awful groan
of their father in his own bedroom;
the half-opened door, the give-away stairs.
Her face at the kitchen window has the look
of someone distracted by what never was.
'C-h-a-r . . .'

The poem should always stand by and for itself but 'The Aunt's Story' brings to mind a few general points which bear upon the intentions and processes of this brief collection of notes on a Belfast upbringing.

When I had originally completed this poem I thought it was simply about one particular experience, translated into a story-line, as 'the' past and present criss-cross and turn into fictional reality. Now I see the poem differently. 'The Aunt's Story' records how personal identity, grounded in language as one's vision of one's self ('*character*'), is not *quite* achieved by the uniformed boy's hesitant deliberations ('C-h-a-r'). The grammar of consciousness is predicated upon inherited and unquestioned ways of seeing and 'being' – The War, the patriarchal male presences, authority. All of these hints and allusions converge into one simple story – of hearing how one says what one says, what one 'sounds like' – the preserved accents of exile, the fictionalised community of the past. When consciousness is reified and made, however benignly, into a problemical figure of amusement, the psychological impact mirrors the era-changing balance of cultural and political power. Poetry registers the flux and subtext at the unpredictable and volatile level of language. Such tension is what makes poetry poetry.

In the early sixties, the setting for 'The Aunt's Story', this kind of self-consciousness was free-floating and non-programmatic. By the nineties, when the poem was rewritten every fibre of cultural and artistic awareness is drenched in demotic sensitivity to such an extent that contemporary literature (and the arts 'in general') are now almost exclusively interpreted (in the academy and *via* the media) in terms of certain pre-emptive categories of post-colonialism, gender, sexuality and race. All too often these categories become self-fulfilling predictions, a kind of intellectual wiring for 'sound-bites'.

In *Literary Englands* (1993) David Gervais, discussing Philip Larkin, John Betjeman and the aftermath of 'England' remarks:

> . . . far from being the option of the sentimentalist, nostalgia has become a living part of our culture, something we may sometimes feel stuck with but not something we can simply wash our hands of. It is in this sense that I think it is possible to think of our England as 'the aftermath of England'.

Somewhat earlier in the same chapter, Gervais draws attention to several books which 'seek to colonise the past in the interests of their own particular version of England':

> What they look back to may vary; what they have in common is the act of looking back. Nostalgia is itself a kind of country, a focus of shared feelings through which we can acknowledge our nationality without relapsing into mere nationalism.

'Nostalgia': *nostos*, return home; *algos*, pain. It is the common condition of many hundreds of thousands (millions?) in these islands of Ireland and Britain. The battle for cultural and political hegemony – who validates and legitimises the 'authentic' version of the past, for which reasons and, most importantly, with what effect on artistic values – should not obscure the dynamic, wayward and unforeseeable power of the imagination to dramatise the irretrievably human consequences and desires of our simply being here, in one place rather than another.

Select Bibliography

ASCHERSON, Neal — *Games with Shadows* 1998

BARDON, Jonathan — *Belfast: An Illustrated History* 1982

BECKETT, Samuel — *Disjecta* 1983

BELL, Sam Hanna — *The Hollow Ball* 1961

BENNET, Ronan — 'An Irish Answer' *The Guardian* 16th July 1994

BROWN, Terence — 'Let's Go To Graceland' in *Studies on the Contemporary Irish Theatre* (eds. G. Genet and E. Hellegouarch) 1991

BRUCE, Steve — *God Save Ulster* 1986
The Edge of the Union 1994

BUCKLAND, Patrick — *A History of Northern Ireland* 1981

CHARTERS, Anne — *The Penguin Book of the Beats* 1992

CLARKSON, Leslie — 'The City and the Country' in *Belfast: The Making of the City 1800–1914* 1983

COLLINS, Brenda — 'The Edwardian City' in *Belfast: The Making of the City 1800–1914* 1983

DAWE, Gerald — *The Lundys Letter* 1985
Sunday School 1991
Heart of Hearts 1995

DIDION, Joan — *Slouching Towards Bethlehem* 1974

FOSTER, John Wilson — 'A Belfast Childhood', *Irish Literary Supplement* Autumn 1989

GERVAIS, David — *Literary Englands* 1993

GRIMBLE, Ian — *Scottish Clans and Tartans* 1973

HARKNESS, David — *Northern Ireland since 1920* 1983

HEANEY, Seamus   *Death of a Naturalist* 1966

KAVANAGH, Patrick   'Poetry Since Yeats: An Exchange of Views', *Tri-Quarterly*, No. 4, 1965

The Letters of John Keats, selected and edited by Stanley Gardner 1965

KEROUAC, Jack   *On the Road* 1958

LARKIN, Philip   *All What Jazz* 1968

LIBERMAN, Alexander   *The Artist in his Studio* 1988

MACMATHUNA, Ciaran   *Traditional Music: Whose Music?* (edited by Peter MacNamee) 1991

MACNEICE, Louis   *Collected Poems* 1991

MAGUIRE, W. A.   *Belfast* 1993

MAHON, Derek   *Selected Poems* 1991
'Poetry in Northern Ireland', *20th Century Studies* November 1970

MELLY, George   *Revolt Into Style* 1989

MONTALE, Eugenio   *The Second Life of Art: Selected Essays* 1992

PARKER, Stewart   *Three Plays for Ireland* 1980
'Me and Jim', *Irish University Review: James Joyce Special Issue* Vol. 12 No. 1. 1982
Dramatis Personae: John Malone Memorial Lecture 1986

POWER, Vincent   *Send 'em Home Sweatin'* 1990

SARTRE, Jean Paul   *Nausea* 1969

WILLIAMS, Carlos William   *Collected Poems: Vol. II 1939–1962* 1991

YORK, Richie   *Van Morrison: Into the Music* 1975

ABOUT THE AUTHOR

GERALD DAWE is the author of *Sheltering Places*, *The Lundys Letter*, *Sunday School* and *Heart of Hearts*. He has been awarded a Major State Award from the Northern Ireland Department of Education, a Bursary for Poetry and The Macaulay Fellowship for Literature from An Chomhairle Ealaion/The Arts Council, Ireland and a Hawthornden International Writers' Fellowship. He lives in Dún Laoghaire and teaches at Trinity College, Dublin.

IMPEDIMENTS
by
Adrian Rice

ISBN : 1 901617 00 9   paperback 32pp
Price : £3

'Adrian Rice has a nice sense of what he is up to as a poet:
I like and admire the way his district and his diction are so
artfully tongue-in-cheek and hand-in-glove.'

SEAMUS HEANEY

'This is a book in plain language about plain people. It shares their
suspicion of excessive speech – of ornamentation, rhetoric, floweriness of
feeling or surface. . . . *Impediments* seems, sadly and genuinely, to
soulsearch on behalf of its community and therefore do it honour.'

RUTH PADEL, *Causeway*

◆

SIGNALS
An anthology of Poetry & Prose
edited by
Adrian Rice

ISBN : 1 901617 02 5   hardback 128pp
ISBN : 1 901617 01 7   paperback 128 pp
Price : £8.95 pbk / £13.95 hbk

Signals – a *Times Educational Supplement* 'Paperback Choice' –
includes new or previously uncollected work from Ian Duhig,
Michael Longley, Glenn Patterson, Catherine Graham, John Kelly,
Douglas Carson, Adrian Rice, Patricia Craig, Robert McLiam Wilson,
Gerald Dawe, Mel McMahon, Martin Lynch, Joan Newmann,
Richard Godden, Tom McCaughren and Mark Roper.

'Schools which struggle with desktop publishing to produce anthologies will
gaze in wonder at the output of Abbey Grammar School, Newry. The school
launched its own press during its Arts week last February and this collection
by the writers who took part in the week, is the stylish, eclectic result.
Perfect for fifth or sixth form libraries.'

GERALDINE BRENNAN, *Times Educational Supplement*

BROKEN DISHES
by
Michael Longley

ISBN : 1 901617 04 1 paperback 32pp
Price : £4
Publication Date : April 1998

'A keeper of the artistic estate,
a custodian of griefs and wonders.'

SEAMUS HEANEY

'His structures have that ease of utterance
which approximations of rhyme and rhythm
do not injure – the true Yeatsian gift.'

PETER PORTER

◆

THE HOME FIRE
by
Mark Roper

ISBN : 1 901617 05 X paperback 32pp
Price : £4
Publication Date : June 1998

'. . . Unusually, Roper has learnt from both Larkin and Heaney,
and if there is hybridization, it has produced a distinctively
original growth . . . those who care about poetry's survival
should keep the cameras trained on his progress.'

CAROL RUMENS, *Fortnight*

'. . . Mark Roper deserves to be considered in the front rank
of Irish poets.'

BILL TINLEY, *Irish Literary Supplement*